the last word

Acknowledgements

Many essays in this volume were published as separate articles in journals. I wish to make acknowledgement to the publishers for permission to reproduce them here. In order to fit them for this publication, I had to alter some of them; their substances, however, remain the same.

Transition (Kampala, Uganda) No. 19 and *East Africa Journal* (Nairobi, Kenya) June, 1965, for: "Can we Correct Literary Barrenness in East Africa?"

The Washington Post Potomac (Washington, D.C., U.S.A.) July 13, 1966, for: "African Students in Washington."

Africa Report (Washington, D.C., U.S.A.) November, 1965, for: "*Weep Not, Child* and *Origin East Africa*."

East Africa Journal (Nairobi, Kenya) June, 1966, for: "What is a Crocodile?" and November, 1966, for: "Negritude: Crying Over Spilt Milk."

Nexus (Nairobi, Kenya) No. 4, for: "Postscript: Dear Leonard Kibera."

Africa Report (Washington, D.C., U.S.A.) October, 1968, for: "African Students are Culturally Deprived."

Busara (Nairobi, Kenya) Vol. I. No. 1 for "Tutuola, son of Zinjanthropus."

TABAN lo LIYONG

the
last
word

CULTURAL SYNTHESISM

modern african LIBRARY

First published in 1969 by the
East African Publishing House P.O. Box 30571, Nairobi

Copyright © Taban lo Liyong 1969

Printed in letterpress by afropress ltd.
P.O. Box 30502, Nairobi, Kenya

CONTENTS

My father, his life and death, my wife, my art, and all that

My father lived and died. Why did he have life at all? No answer. But, uninvited, he came. He clung to life for a number of years. During those years he established some relationships with a number of people. His parents for example. Then his wives. And his children. And grandchildren. He had friends, also. He was, besides, a government item: a tax payer, a census figure, a legal party and, finally, an entry in the death register.

When he died, he might have been sixty or so years. According to the Christian (Justinian?) calendar. Another calendar could have reckoned the same length of time as one thousand years. Another: one day. The division of time into years, months, weeks, days, hours, minutes, seconds, moments, etc. is an arbitrary creation. Once the continuum time was arbitrarily imposed, the impositions were endowed with powers. These powers became regulators for man's life. Very dictatorial. Men have learnt to run and account for each moment of their life. You have to be a Buddhist to enjoy timelessness in the tranquillity of nirvana.

In the summer (there we meet time again) of 1964 (!) I was studying in the University of North Carolina,

Chapel Hill. I wrote an article called, "My History is Yours Too". When I gave this to a North Carolinian to read, he commented after reading, that it was all "like a kite": with wings, legs, tail, which could not be brought under control. It should have been coordinated, controlled, or sequential. My essay was unordered. For people who are chasing or saving time, it was a waste of time; for those who look forward to an essay written on the smooth line after either Aristotle's 'beginning, middle and an end' or the journalistic 'who, what, when, why, and how' my work was arbitrary or nonconformist. I admit the charges. So what? Isn't each writer an arbitrary maker, ordering or reordering the world? Isn't each reader a naturalized subject who submits to each author's dictatorship at his own peril and continues the relationship as long as it is mutually beneficial? Isn't the tyranny of an author as good as that of a musician, a lover, a parent, or anybody's? You see, freedom and tutelage exist at the same time. You are free from one thing in order to come under the dominion of another. Most of us have been to many wedding feasts; some of us don't care for any such nonsense; some never get invited. But, if I were on my way to a wedding feast, and were offered a mariner's tale, I would forgo the feast. Such chances never come one's way more than once.

I am going to tell you the story of my father's death. By and by. But I am a dictator; I hold the gavel. While it is in my hand, I shall wield a heavy dictatorial power. No need turning over the pages to see how much longer you have to submit. For I might never tell you about my father at all. On the other hand, I might. No knowing. My advice is: enjoy each moment of the time. If you *must* rush away for an appointment, or a wedding feast, go.

In Chapel Hill, North Carolina, I used to do my writings in a coffeehouse called Carolina Coffee Shop. (Here in Iowa, Sug's Maid-rite is my writing Coffee Shop. I mention these by way of showing my gratitude.) Each writer must be able to discover a congenial atmosphere for literary production.

After I had been in school for some years and had grown up (whatever that means to a person who knows not when he was born) my father thought I should get married. He, a polygamist with three wives, saw no reason why it should take so long for him to get a daughter-in-law through me. Three or four daughters-in-law, possibly. After all, his parents and grandparents all the way back as far as memory could report, had never had less than one wife. It was inconceivable for the pattern to be broken. It wouldn't, I assured him. For I am going to marry an African, then an American (Red Indian), then a European, then a Japanese or a Chinese or an Indian, and finally a Maori or a Fijian. No joke. And, by the way, I write this by way of an advertisement for myself. If any girl has the inclination or is sure she is interestet in being a polygamist's wife, let her place a collect call, person to person, to the number I shall give in this story. A call is a promise.

When I was still a village boy, before I went to school, that is, I used to draw all sorts of things on the compound. If Pablo Ruiz Picasso had seen them (in the early forties) he would have envied me. And when I went to school, I started to expand my art to mural paintings, sign-writing, design, and woodcarving. I was the school artist. When I was young, very young, I possessed a carving, the Wakamba carvings so widely known now. It was the bust of a girl with breasts, and brass neckbands. I loved it, had it with me all the times: time for bath or time for bed. Later, the owner came and took it away from me. I cried and cried and possibly vowed to make some carvings later by myself and for myself. I did. After I had made many wooden and clay heads, busts and ceramic pieces, my fame spread and neighbours came to see. Soon, they began to speak. A decade or so ago, they said, there lived a man, the best artist they had known, who used to make the things I was making. But each time he married himself a wife, she died. So for him, marriage was instantly followed by the death of the bride. The moral my father was to draw from the neighbours' concern was this: If this son of yours continues in this path, old man, you won't have a daughter-in-law, consequently, no grandchildren; your lineage ends with this artist son of yours. Forced to choose between art and daughters-in-law, my father, who could not conceive of immortality other than through procreation, acted. One evening, when I returned from school tired and hungry, I found all my art creations burning, and my father supervising the destruction. That Philistine!

Had I been my father, I would have done the same.

When I came for college studies in America in 1962, my object was to study Political Science. After a brilliant B.A. I hoped to get another brilliant M.A., and later, an equally brilliant Ph.D. Then I would go to lecture Political Science in Makerere College, Uganda. I would be the most brilliant political scientist in Makerere, doing finer, keener, original and more advanced work than Professor Ali Mazrui who now holds the Headship of the Political Science Department there. I understand he is more conservative and traditional than he thinks in an age and among people who want radicalism even from scholars. In fact, I doubt whether the Africa of today has a wide room for the important

10

(known otherwise as objective) scholar in the Social Sciences.

"Ali Mazrui is an Aristotelian. The Aristotelians are invariably pedestrians: they crawl on the terrain, painstakingly taking note of its twists and turns. Like snails, they sometimes have a hard time trying to push their weights from one place to another; have great difficulties trying to circumvent an obstacle — they have to feel their ways around a problem, therefore covering a long unnecessary distance. But this is where they derive their immense pleasure from: the occupation of covering a large distance in order to prove that something is as it is or as it is not.

"These Aristotelians should be made to tabulate, to assemble facts and information for their intellectual betters, the Platonists: the ones who enunciate principles, who have an eagle's perspective of the landscape and who can sense where the hills and snags are. It is the Platonists who set the world going; it is the Aristotelians who maintain it. The Aristotelians are as important as the mechanics; and the Platonists the designers. In truth, IN TRUTH, the human conception of the world, and that is the realer world to man, was created by Platonists. The disciples (Aristotelians) have continually written commentaries upon commentaries on this phenomenon; they have popularised it. These liaison men are needed, surely, to translate matters transcendental to other Aristotelians and also the populace, subaristotelians. Mazrui has tried to translate some Platonism and more Aristotelianism to the subaristotelians basking in the tropics. In other words, he has been catering to the popular more than the rigidly scholarly. Perhaps because of the low level of intellectual involvement in East Africa and Africa generally, he has at most times occupied himself with the transmission of messages rarefied, incomprehensible, paltry. The themes chosen, their exploration, the quality of the mind at work, do not satisfy. Academic trappings — footnotes, allusions, etc., almost rescue the works.

"He tries to display his bravery far from the arena where he should be immediately engaged. He is misdirecting his energy. On Swahili and Uganda he has written, on Tanzania versus East Africa he has written, on the fall of Nkrumah he has written; on Kenyatta-Mboya-Odinga he has not yet written, on the poor in Kenya he keeps quiet. Nkrumah's government which he criticizes was the government of the 'verandah boys'. If Nkrumah was a dictator, he was a democratic dictator, dictating for the good of the many as opposed to the interests of the selfish few 'been-tos': that cancerous black bourgeoisie rising fast all over Africa and fattening on the sweat of the duped people, a homicide squad filled by politicians, traders, professors.

"Chinua Achebe finally realised that the devils in our midst are worse vampires that those from afar whom we can sup with from a distance; ours look brotherly but have poisoned teeth. In a time when Africa is involved in the establishment of a new order, ought not those who have eyes to see coming abominations help open the eyes of the others? Ought not those with intelligence warn us about present dangers? Ought not those who have a comparative view try to adjust things to a general universal pace? Ought not those with a historical perspective tell us which paths we should avoid? Ought the enlightened join in a conspiracy with the powers that be in order to enjoy a co-existence perennial and inimical, quite oblivious of the revolutions they are generating? Ought our so-called intellectuals waste valuable psychic energy glorifying days past, flogging dead horses and other such trivia?

"Rather than ask whether Nkrumah had not failed us, we should ask if we, his dream, have not failed him, whether we have not failed to sustain that noble dream. Were we not the people chasing after our Ph.D.'s, writing 'academic' articles, checking how many i's are dotted or not dotted; how many t's are crossed or not crossed in a given paper? Meanwhile trusting that as before so today Nkrumah the Osagyefo will lick them? Forgetting that they had meanwhile re-assembled their forces and forged new techniques? Instead of enrolling as soldiers we became objective audiences of our own tragedy! Inexonerable ones.

"A man's stature is determined by the ratio between what he had set out to do and how much of that he achieved. Nkrumah's thoughts, actions, and life, have altered radically the world's rating of the blacks everywhere. Whoever gives man dignity is called Messiah. In that context, Nkrumah, our Redeemer, our Osagyefo, is greater than Christ.

"Ought, in other words, our Aristotelians menace the populace with aggregation of irrelevants instead of confronting other Aristotelians and the powers that be? In other words, ought our Aristotelians mistake the politicians for Platonists? So that they (the Aristotelians) become the 'intellectual' arm while the police and secret service are the panga arm, of the governments? In other words, should our intellectuals (mostly Aristotelians) not become critics (=evaluators) of everything especially in our own countries where any Biafras or cultural revolutions will surely shed the blood of those we love?

"African wealth-grabbing, women-chasing, renascent masochist; politicians and bureaucrats; misguided scholars (they do not know that the so-called 'academic objectivity' they parade as a mark of distinction, that the so-called 'scientific method', evolved as a compromise between the pure intellect that sheds light on everything and an aristocratic establishment which fears to be exposed. If the scholars loved their works and did not want to be rounded up and exiled or killed at the stakes or *auto-da-fe,* they were allowed to work so long as they showed due reverence to the powers that be, handled (if at all) touchy (to the powers, of course) matters very impersonally and at a distance. In other words, here were eunuchs living in harems. Without emotions, in impersonal ways, they took care of their masters' possessions and like the good butlers they were, they kept dark matters secret but would bark like bitches and bits like bulldogs at the 'enemies' of their masters. In other words, scholars were to localize their works, inquiries, among the affected objects, were not to trace the courses the effects went through to arrive at their destination, never bothered about the very causes of all the ills: theirs was to observe the manifestations, describe the phenomena there and then and earn a prize and be praised; step outside that and point an accusing finger at Tyrannus and all is lost for them as far as the world was concerned, they were mad: criminals, traitors, enemies of the people, etc. I have very low opinion of these academic people. You need a Karl Marx to show them a thing or two.

" (The present crop of educated Africans aspired to the new life. All their upbringing was a preparation for some cosy place somewhere in the government or industry, but surely in the high class occupied by executives here and

M.P.'s there. After the expulsion of the foreign powers, and when we wanted 'to do things in our way', one is surely a 'traitor' if one abandons all aspirations, all easy living, all good quarters, the support of 'our' ways of doing things; and one adopts instead an independent outlook. It takes courage to do that. It is a great sacrifice to one's purse, one's relatives (poor), one's friends. Few people are capable of that. A man can do it.)

"Mazrui is an Aristotelian; Nkrumah is a Platonist. Nkrumah dreamed a free continent. Both his critics and admirers are playing under the canopy of his dream. Mazrui credits Nkrumah more with taking advantage of the time for his continental dream. But Mazrui seems not to realize that, if it comes to that, time is always ripe for something for those who know how to read the signs aright. One could take advantage of the time and manoeuvre oneself into the Chair of the English Department in an African University, for example.

"Mazrui's first article about Nkrumah's fall published in *Transition* is what one could expect from a graduate research assistant. His second article, hammered out after many months as a reply to tougher questions than those within his ken, was sickeningly meek in tone, full of humility and contrition and neurosis. It was a letter addressed to the gallery, to wit Nkrumah. With much show of sentiment, lachrymal functioning, he exhibited that rarest form of contrition known only to the many unnerved would-be assassins of the Osagyefo. A confessional. That article is therefore Mazrui's act of piety, at once lyrical and singular and deriving its life from the inner cords; the tone and atmosphere are subdued, ritualistic: an atonement with the spirit of Africa. Good for the glands. But he did not touch on the most pertinent problem: the role of international politics and economics in the reduction of Ghana to poverty. Can one who really wants to be taken intellectually seriously leave out international economic conspiracy in the Ghana and African tragedy? One can cry till one has filled Lake Victoria with tears and yet not matter intellectually. I put it to Mazrui that Nkrumah could have been more ostentatious, more egotistical, could have initiated more economic and political projects and Nkrumah's Ghana would still be existing to-day as strong economically as any African nation, had there been no western plot on Ghana which saw its effective way to success through economic and other manipulations. cf. Haiti, Liberia, Portugal.

"Those who say Nkrumah failed Ghana should do some comparative work. Mazrui professes he is good at such a thing but does not show it in action when most needed. Which African nations were then doing better for the masses of their people? For example, was the plight of the ordinary Ugandan then better than that of the ordinary Ghanaian? Were Liberian citizens, Ethiopian citizens, Egyptian citizens having a better time, and more freedom than Ghanaians? Between Ghana and South Africa which government deserved overthrowing by the C.I.A., the British and French services, if it was for the sake of throwing out a dictator?

"Ghana is said to have entered into great debts, but are there no governments in comparatively worse debts than Ghana was? Are there no 'unimaginative' economic plannings besides those we blame Nkrumah for? Don't governments have priority projects and don't they adopt austerity measures to tide them over hard times? Instead of looking at African problems as *sui generis* we should look at them as particular manifestations of the general order. Oh these intellectual vultures. Waiting for the fall of another leader in order to rehash another article on the future African Mao, deriving cues from the international press.

"If he wants to be taken seriously, Mazrui should pitch his ball above the reach of the undergraduates and engage in a man to man talk with celebrities past and present. Nobody can succeed in enlightening the rabble, so there is no need to waste one's little store of pearls before them, there is no need for one to preen oneself before them if one could do higher things. He who enters into a common controversy with the undergraduates is to blame if he wins or is bloodied. The very exposure of oneself to such an attack is a lack of stature. I am sure the pages of *Transition* can carry articles of greater intellectual worth written right there in Kampala. Once in a while, it will be psychedelically desirable to come across a Kantian rigidity and near-incomprehensibility.

"It is also one's duty as an enlightened one, a duty one owes to the taxpayers whose money enabled one to acquire the knowledge and the covetted position, to help direct the ship. One should determine the direction the ship is to take; one should retire inept pilots; one should pull the siren when the ship is headed for a wreck. One has to bring the rulers up willy-nilly whether one is a Platonist or an Aristotelian."

My first semester's work was brilliant. A's. Second semester: A's. and a D. I'll tell you why I got a D. I got it in Music Appreciation. A graduate of the Juilard School of Music known by the Italian name of Pellegrini had difficulties establishing himself as a teacher. In the last week, Pellegrini gave us a list of the compositions we would have to identify for the finals. Portions of the works would be played over the record player, and we would have to write who composed the work, and what the composition was. The way we were going to subvert the American educational system was this: one of the students we made our leader. He assigned numbers, one to ten, to the works. Each number was represented by one finger, beginning from the smallest left finger. So when a record was played, and it was Beethoven's Symphony Number 5, the leader, sitting in the middle of the front row, would raise his pointing finger of the right hand (number 7), and so on. This method worked very well for those who used it. I didn't. Either I lost count, or my puritan upbringing might have constrained me through the dictatorship of the subconscious. Whatever it was, I wavered between cheating and relying on my own ability. The confusion resulted in a poorer performance than I would have done if I had concentrated on either method. (I resolved afterwards that since education is an arbitrary tradition, I am going to be as arbitrary in dealing with it). (Perhaps we were not subverting the American educational system? There is no reason why one couldn't go to school expressly to score D's and F's.)

My uncle (on my mother's side) had a musical instrument *(lekembe)* which I used to play competently when I was still young (the early forties again.) When he went away, he took it away with him. Since then I have been knocking at the music door.

In the next year at College, I got A's and a few B's again. I was in the honour rolls both years.

Then I met a girl and decided to get married. After all, I am my father's son. The marriage was to take place in the end of the summer of 1964. The time came (inevitably), I got married and lost my academic excellence.

My father was pleased. At last his son was going to be a man. After this first marriage, he would as surely get another wife. Polygamy for ever and ever. And, possibly at the back of his mind, now that the son was no longer making those nonsensical but deadly carvings, these daughters-in-law wouldn't die.

He worked hard at home (for acquiring my African wife, you remember?), paid the bride-price and met the parents of my bride, enjoyed himself very much, and also saw my wife in the shape of her identical twin sister. Now that his problem child was married, and all things were going well, he would have his grand-children, my father's last task in life was finished. So abandoning resistance to diseases, he consented to die in that same summer.

Perhaps I shouldn't have married just then.

My mother, whose responsibilities are as extensive as those of Hera, knew she would be needed for quite a while. Her existence is a necessity for her two daughters, and her son, and her grandchildren, daughters-in-law and sons-in-law. Despite a dislocated right shoulder, she is functioning with double the energy she had before her husband died. She will live for a long time yet. Unless I make another mistake.

In 1962 while still in Uganda I found myself torn between two scholarships and subjects of studies. I had won a scholarship for studying political science in the United States. I had also won a scholarship for studying art in Nairobi College. With my father still alive, my choice was obvious. I rationalized it then on the ground that I had been a practical politician helping to drive the British out and my studies of political science would merely be a continuation. Moreover political science is more intellectual than mere art, so the tune went.

The news of my father's death reached me in North Carolina. I had just finished the first session of summer school, subjects: European systems of government and cultural anthropology (my minor was to be sociology). When I enrolled for the second session, I took a graduate course in Shakespeare, taught by the Harvard-trained professor they have down there; and the first part of American literature — that intellectually richest period comprising the puritans, the metaphysicians, the transcendentalists and such figures as Emerson, Thoreau, Whitman, Hawthorne, Melville.

Hip hip hip! Hurray! Hurray! Hurray! Three Cheers! For dad is dead. And with his death is removed that ruling against my studying art.

English was thenceforth my major. Written English is an art. My long-time aim was to go back to art. I could not approach it directly as my father's dictatorship still hovered so near me. I felt like Hamlet's mother after the King's death. Only in my case, I allowed myself a longer period between the death of my father and my marriage to his enemy art.

My bride was still in England. Marriage was impending. Marriage is a social commitment. I had plenty of thought on society (why not, after all those social science courses taken and papers written) and commitment and arbitrariness connected with them. These thoughts I wrote down into a 400-page foolscap paper ms. in the Carolina Coffee Shop. When I left political science for art, I had to get the permission of my subconscious by lying (plausibly) that I needed more knowledge of English in order to revise my thoughts then so rawly jotted down. That was a bluff. Those original thoughts of mine appear best in their rough apparels. The stuff and the manner of presentation cannot be separated without introducing weaknesses. But I locked that manuscript away and went on writing other things and publishing them, supposedly to pave the way for that *magnum opus*. Since then I have written poems, articles, stories, criticisms. What you are reading is another of the pathpavers.

Possibly, the impending marriage generated the energy for the thoughts and the writing of them. If my ideas were favourable to society my manuscript should be rosy, if the manuscript is gloomy then I doomed society. We have to wait till I 'revise' or 'rewrite' and publish that work.

But, my father died, I changed to English. In 1965 I was already looking for a graduate school. I chose the University of Iowa, the Writers' Workshop. One of the major determinants was this: while working for an M.A. in creative writing students are required to study another language or art. I went for art: drawing, sculpture, painting, photography, printmaking, ceramics.

Dad is dead. If my wives will want to die, defying modern medicine, my art will not be blamed for it.

If I acted arbitrarily in detaining you this long, I have no apology to give. For what social thing is not arbitrary? There is nothing beyond the arbitrary. That is the alpha and the omega of it.

Can we correct literary barrenness in East Africa?

To be an African these days means to be many things. Those who deceived themselves that we are not men have now changed their minds; the struggle and attainment of independence smashed the myth. Our humanhood is no longer questioned. But our manhood is. In every field of human endeavour, we are expected to participate. Then our achievements are compared to those of participants from the old outside world. Within the young black world too, national pride is great enough to engender a competitive spirit. In literary production, some African states have more, but the overall picture shows one at a glance that much is still to be desired. Be that as it may, the nations which have writers are very proud. This is what I found out one day when a group of us Africans studying at Howard University, Washington, D.C. were discussing literary works. The group was comprised of Africans from the French-speaking section, Ghana, Nigeria, South Africa (not Verwoerdians though, I assure you) and East Africans. The Nigerians waxed grand talking about their Achebes, Ekwensis, Njokwus, Clarks, Soyinkas, Okaras, and, would have bored us stiff with the catalogue if somebody had not interrupted. I cannot remember very well where he was from; he might have been a Ghanaian. He reminded the Nigerians that they have an Amos Tutuola, too. That shut up their mouths. Just as well.

Though it hurt my national pride, inwardly, I could not help admitting that Nigeria with her imperfect census, has definitely the greatest number of writers. The South Africans spoke next. Some of them were loud, others plaintive. I shook my head and muttered: these people will never stop complaining.

When they were forced to explain why all their writers do not write from inside South Africa, they could not give adequate explanations. Harder still was the question: do you still claim that Zeke Mphahlele in Chemchemi, Nairobi; Bloke Modisane, Lewis Nkosi, Noni Jabavu, and Alfred Hutchinson, all in England; and Peter Abrahams in Jamaica, are South African writers? An exile in an exile. He is a part of the country he is in at any moment. I later thought that by jumping the Apartheid curtains, these "exiles" have transcended national (or sectional) feelings and become citizens of the wider world. One South African reminded us that their writers abroad had first learnt their language in South Africa. Well, we shrugged our shoulders and prompted the French to speak. Their leader buttoned up his Parisian suit carefully and said they were philosophers. That was cheeky. We became indignant. Philosophy is not part and parcel of a Parisian suit, we told him. He urged us to calm down. We demanded proof of their philosophy. He simply said: Negritude. I challenged him. Aime Cesaire of the West Indies coined that word. I said no. Sedar Senghor popularised it. I said that that word was in existence long before anybody could have suspected Senghor would be born; Charles Lamb had used it as early as 1822 in his essay called "The Praise of Chimney-Sweepers." He wrote this:

> "I like to meet a sweep ... one of those tender
> voices, blooming through their first *negritude* ....
> I have a kingly yearning toward these dim specks —
> poor blots — innocent blackness — ... I reverence
> these young Africans of our own growth — ...
> preach (ing) a lesson of patience to mankind."

This Francified African was cultured enough to drop the Negritude stuff. He asked me if I had heard of Camara Laye. "Yes", I said, "the writer of *L'Enfant Noir?*" He nodded. "I read that one as long ago as 1957". If he had thought I was that illiterate, he deceived himself. He next challenged me about Mongo Beti. I read his books, in translation, too. I did not want to be accused of dominating the discussion group. So I looked to the right.

The next chair was empty. A Sierra Leone girl was supposed to come and tell us about Willam Conton's *The African* but never showed up. It was the Ghanaian's turn then. He had brought a copy of *Ghana* with him. No doubt, Ghana has the greatest biography (if a biography could be great) in this work by the Redeemer, President Kwame Nkrumah. He said the president has written three other books, one being a work of philosophy called *Consciencism.* Somebody got cynical. The Ghanaian was asked, "Is the literary world there the monopoly of the President?" He said no. They had poets and sociological writers. This latter answer fell on deaf ears; the cynic had scored a tactical victory. I wanted to question this Ghanaian more, but shied away. You see, it was my turn to talk next. I was to talk about the literary climate in my country: East Africa. As you well know, we do not have much to show. I cleared my voice and assumed the seriousness of a professor emeritus. (My public speaking professor had emphasized that to us: If you do not have much to say, look big; people will give you grades for the speech, the substance, and the manner. Your manner will compensate for your lack of substance.) I said we have a very authoritative anthropological work on the Gikuyu tribe; Mau Mau reminiscences; a few political works elaborating the concept called African Socialism; some political complaints, a few tales and ... I halted. There were shufflings of feet on the wooden floor. Somebody cleared his throat. "Literature man, tell us about literature." I mentioned the name Rebeca Njau. They asked what she has written. I could not remember. I told them of Grace Ogot. Certainly they have read her stories in Rajat Neogy's *Transition*. Some said yes, some no. I told them off. I am not responsible for their ignorance. But surely James Ngugi's two novels should be popular with them. One said he had ordered a copy but it had not yet arrived. Another said the library does not even have a copy. I got disgusted. I stood up to walk out. The fact is, all in all, I had contributed nothing.

I walked to my apartment, threw my bookcase on the the bed and sat next to it. I then held my big head between my powerful hands. I squeezed it, and squeezed it hard, till it thought. When thoughts came, they poured like tropical rain: big and fast. I pulled out a pencil and a paper and wrote fast, capturing every drop of thought. These were precious thoughts, the vintage of a fertile vineyard. If they were taken to that marriage feast at Cana, they would have won first place.

Taste them.

"I sing a song to Thee, Oh Country. It is a song to thy poetic mountains. A song dedicated to thy symphonic valleys and prosaic lakes which hold fast the people.

This is a song of lamentations, do you hear? It is a song worthy of thy modern-music waterfalls. Waterfalls worthy of the inspiration of odes to a passing beauty in face of the overflowing civilization-nursing and time-defying natural streams.

"Thy immensity is worthy the lofty vocabulary of a master; now thou boasts of many mute inglorious Miltons. Lacking that, thou should have borne an Uncle Remus. But that is not yet. Without Uncle Remus would it not have done to have even an Amos Tutuola? Tutuola lives; is only one, and far in his jungles.

"Epics of Kintu-type await encasement in eternity of Homeric *Iliad* or *Odyssey*. Now with every passing second the memory grows old and weak, becoming in the long run blank. Perhaps the fables could get a Grimm's treatment, if no Aesop could be found or hired to give them precision. Many there are that float in the air being blown away each minute while few are imperfectly pinned down in black and white. Might anthropology capture for us in hard uninteresting frames food worthy the nourishment and excitation of joyous wits? That is, if nothing better could be found? When will the Nile basin find a Dickens or a Conrad? Or a Mark Twain? Or a Joyce Cary? Is Rudyard Kipling coming to Mowgli our national parks? Will the muses living on the Mountain Moons; will the dwellers of Kere-Nyaga; will the skyscraping Kilimanjaro, acquire lyricists, poets, musicians to sing to them? When come you Omar Khayyam? Timbuktu is dead, Mali is flat. Zanzibar is dead, Tanzania not so fragrant. No more flute to be piped from the island for coastal dancers. Oh Zanzibar, where the Saint-Devil Okello did good-evil work in the field with one stroke *a la* tale of two islands, give us the writer to paint the woes and joys of the day.

Kisenyi awaits a Zola to give it fictional immortality;
Katwe an Alan Paton for a John Kumalo setting. This
sentence is a tribute to you Robert Ruark. You wrote
Uhuru and about Mau Mau. We have not. We ban you
for writing. We do not scribble, and call ourselves great.
We hurry to Top Life to be lifted up in ecstasy of its
rhythmic Uhuru songs, and drag ourselves back to
Makerere to drowse over Colin Legum. What a descent!
What impressions really register in our scholars'
minds which are not forceful enough to demand dictation
on paper? We go hunting. And we hunt elephants,
simbas, kifaroos, zebras, giraffes, impalas, gazelles.
But Hemingway writes a safari. Conrad and Kurtz and
Congo trading companies and civilizing missions. Sir Rider
Haggard and Gagool and King Solomon's Mines. Who
will turn the record over and give us the music on the
reverse side? Have we no Nigerian forests for a Tutuola
Journey? Is our traditional life blown and gone west by
a strong eastern wind? Yet there is a harmattan in
Nigeria. We squatted too long to form and preserve
Ibo societies of Achebe's specialization. Baker, Stanley,
Emin Pasha, Livingstone monopolised, yet they
monopolised the narration of history-marring-creating
black-white encounters and forgot the African's discovery
on his own soil of the white. Mutesa (I mean the first),
your descendants neither dramatize your greatness
nor your wisdom-folly. Their mouths are shut.
They drink tongue-tying double Haig or Haig and Haig;
Haig straight and rounded and rocky scotches. The
story-telling mwenge is forgot. Perhaps our eloquence
returns with legal waragi. Kilimanjaro, oh, mighty
Kilimanjaro, the only tribute paid thee, the only
inspiration thou inspireth is an alien Roman Julius
Caesar tale Julius translated into a crossbreed tongue.

Patterson's snake that has smoke and runs on rail is still only in Tsavo man eaters. A Danish Saga called *Out of Africa* came from Karen Blixen's pen. She was a baroness; no royalty of Uasin Gishu or white snowless islands. Perhaps the Masai may claim the lordship. Huxley gave us a legion. Depend upon the Huxleys. That is a chosen clan which gives. They produce in California. They produce in Kenya. We have a Mrs. Ogot. Yes, a Mrs. Manhood for holding the plumes is with the fair sex. Name them: Noni Jabavu, Efua Sutherland, Grace Ogot. Bravo to the sex that produces. To you dames I take off my hat.

"Is it the 'whiteness' of the teeth which makes humans laugh or sing? Ask p'Bitek. One thing I know. We need more *Lak Tar*.

"We need Ngugis in plural to do a la Guma job between a capital letter and a period. Come, come songsters, work our sentiments and emotions, and instincts hot and cool. Weave your flirting, flitting yarns on natural objects. Pour forth your hearts' contents of a moral-creating-destroying fashion-wise world.

"Ezekiel, Ezekiel, you saw the wheel, in the middle of the air. Will you help, Ezekiel to resurrect our manly spirits to see the wheel of thought and imagination? Ezekiel Mphahlele (it sounds poetic: Mphahlele Ezekiel) teach us to write. Open our mouths. Else we choke with lumps of thoughts. Else we go migrating in search of inspiration to Mbari. Else we cut Ulli Beier into two and leave Nigeria with the legs.

"We want more. But we do not even have any yet. Could we find an alchemist? An alchemist to change Moore, Gerald Moore, into a tribesman to give us another Mbari? Moore will you teach us only to comment?

Only to edit? And not to compose? Too many commentators these days.

"You have heard it said we have no publishers; but I say unto you, the amateur and the professional, go to Bethwell Ogot's *East Africa Journal* or to Rajat Neogy's Olympic *Transition*; you will find field enough to rally, jump, hurdle, sprint, scribe, spin, sit, sip, meditate, mediate...

"Drama school? Yes. Drama diploma? Yes. National cultural theatre? Yes. Playwrights? Yet. Ours is the physical training only, the mental training to compose is the prerogative of the temperate climate. Well....

"Poor muses. You chose the wrong mountains. Ours seem not to be Parnassusses. Is it time which is not yet in joint? Are you uncomfortable in your new abodes? Or do you receive no sacrifices? Yet we boast prolification of all-knowing witch-doctors. Those the Gods mark for their own die young. Dwellers of the mountains spare our bablers. Give them time. They will learn the language. They will come in procession. They are coming: Homer in khaki shorts; Virgil in monkey toga; Dante in a witch-doctor's garb; Shakespeare who speaks a little Karamojong, less Agikuyu, Swahili and Runyankore; a Milton without the eye handicap; a T. S. Eliot who knows Etesot. Wait. Let me see how far away they now are approaching. I mean the black orpheuses. They are...."

Pardon me reader. When inspiration had just struck me about the black orpheuses, and before I could write whatever my muse dictated, Lucy, my wife came into the apartment. She gave me a kiss and demanded to know how my day was. I went on explaining it. After some time, I remembered I had a sentence left incomplete. I took out the paper and pencil and started to write. No thought came. My muse had taken flight during our family formalities. I got mad with my wife and myself. If my wife had not come, definitely the greatest lament on East Africa's literary barrenness would have been written. My wife, seeing the change that had come over me, tried to comfort me. I told her she had done a worse thing than Carlyle's dog who burnt his manuscript. I forced into her hands that fragment of thought. She read it; admired it. After apologizing for her interruption of my train of thought, she suggested that I should now become practical, and discover the reasons for this barrenness, why we need writers, and what could be done to spark interest in literary production. Seeing that my Parnassian muse had deserted me, and realizing that it would be foolish to cry over what I had lost, I settled down to do what she said. So long as man dreams, it is all right if he does it on the mountain heights; but when he wants to solve practical problems, he has to come down to earth.

Ezekiel Mphahlele says that no novel can be written by a non-white in South Africa because of the oppressive political climate existing there. A writer cannot get that peace of mind which is necessary for sustaining a creation when he has to mind about passes, curfews, treason trials, house arrests, works, angers, and whatever infernal tortures the gods of apartheid forge. Lewis Nkosi takes issues with this excuse. That is their domestic quarrel; I do not want to meddle in it; we have our own problems. The question I ask my fellow East Africans is: Why don't we have writers?

I blame the British. The education they came to offer was aimed at recruiting candidates for a Christian Heaven and eliminating others for a Christian Hell;

they sought to teach clerks, teachers, servants, and administrators. Culturally, they stood aloof. They were so high up in their culture (I pity those Englishmen and women who had to practise a forced middle-class life in Africa before going back to their natural life in Cheapside, Birmingham, Soho, or wherever they might have come from) that they had to deal with the primitive Africans in their low cultures through indirect contacts. The two cultures were kept apart. Not only that, the British went about castrating the Africans. Culturally our dances, including songs, became Satanic. We had to sing poorly translated meaningless hymns without experientally felt emotion. Culturally, the French attempt at assimilation was more beneficial. Although the French West Indians and West Africans later rose against the mockery of equality in assimilation by dreaming up a myth called negritude, nobody can deny that the prolific output of literature up-to-date by these new "Frenchmen" is connected with rejection of cultural assimilation and re-orientation to their rediscovered romantic life.

Because the British are a practical-minded people, we became practical-minded too. If they had followed the Romantics they would have given us more culture and more Joyce Carys; but they continued a colonizing race giving us Lord Lugards. Poetry-writing and the art of fiction were not taught us though we debated and reasoned. This led directly to early writings which were of a quarrelsome nature; political grievances (about land, mostly) and answering back the white racist charges through pamphlets, and biographies and anthropological works. Such were the writings from Kenya. A short list of works by Kenyans of the older order and the present shows that there has been no change, apart from Ngugi's and Ogot's shift to the use of the short story and novel for expressing those important ideas. Jomo Kenyatta's *Facing Mount Kenya* (1938), as everyone knows, is mostly an anthropological study of the Gikuyu by a Gikuyu who wanted to justify his people's ways and reprove the British; *The People of Kenya Speak for Themselves* (1955) by Koinange was an effort at presenting the African's case to people in the United States; Josiah Kariuki's *Mau Mau Detainee* (1963) is a slice of a biography and Mau Mau; Tom Mboya's *Freedom and After* (1963) is an autobiography of a politician after Kwame Nkrumah's *Ghana*. Gatheru's *Child of Two Worlds* (1964) is the first glimpse we have of the life story of that very increasing vanguard of cultural contact — the Africans who marry Europeans, Americans, Russians, Indians; *Weep Not Child* (1964) and *The River Between*, by James Ngugi, as we all know, are fictional treatment of the Kenya problems.

In Uganda, Sir Apolo Kaggwa was a prolific writer as well as subject for writings. He was an authority on Buganda ways, traditions, and also a storyteller. *The Tales* of Sir Apolo; *The Customs of Buganda; The Book of Baganda, Banyoro, Bakoki, Batoro, Banyankole Kings* (1912) (with the title in Luganda), are some of his writings. Ham Mukasa wrote *Uganda's Katikiro in England*, which is an official account of Apolo Kaggwa's visit to the coronation of His Majesty King Edward VII in 1904. Another literary figure we have after these is Prince Dr. Akiki K. Nyabongo, the brother of the Omukama of Toro. He studied both in America and England. He refuted western disparagement of Africa in his book bearing the pegulistic title of *Africa Answers Back* (1936); he also went about story telling in *The Bisoro Stories* (1937) and gave a story of the

Black/White encounter in *The Story of An African Chief*. (It is also the theme of David Rubadiri's best poem about "Stanley meets Mutesa".) This scholar and writer is still alive; he lives in Toro. A third writer is Ernest Balintuma Kalibala who while in America wrote *Nakaima and The Clayman, and other African Folktales* (1946), and later translated some of Sir Apolo Kaggwa's Luganda works into English. M. B. Nsimbi is a Muganda linguist and story teller of great enthusiasm. Recently David Cook has brought out an anthology called *Origin East Africa*.

This short survey shows that after reading the fables, biographies, and political works we do not have much else to read for relaxation and enjoyment. Our intellectual leadership has been left to the politicians.

Our citizens of Asian origin have been taking more care of family businesses than engaging in literary works. Yet back in India and Pakistan, Indian literature in English is growing. If the Pope can now discuss such touchy matters as birth control, I see no reason why the Aga Khan and other leaders of Asian religious communities do not search for ways of releasing their followers into the life of twentieth century in East Africa. Our young citizens will have to take definite strides into modern life. They have much to contribute towards our cultural bounty.

Our political leaders have done their best to liberate us. We now need writers to liberate us culturally and through ideas. They will be the ones to revive, maintain and found our culture for us. The importation of text books from Britain is the importation of British cultural ideas into lands where they do not fit, and are not understood. It appears that so long as the Uganda Bookshop brought us Shakespeare and Dickens, we were content. This, too, led to our literary barrenness. Those very ideas could be expressed, and expressed better by our own people.

There is a class of detestable two-legged creatures called specialists — the so-called specialists on Africa. They are detestable, so our social scientists tell us, because most of the time they are ignorant of what they profess to specialize in and because they engage in ideological propaganda and controversies; they give things names, they condemn this and approve that, they predict this and introduce problems and conflicts and confusions where there were none before. All the time they claim they are interpreting Africa. The curse is that our readers tend to believe them. Or if they do not, they have no other works to consult in order to discover the facts or truths. What we need now are dedicated East Africans to interpret East Africa, and Africa, and the world. That is why we need writers.

The clashes between Western, African and Asian cultures which are taking place in East Africa are some of the finest subjects for writing. They are as suitable for the fictional writer as for the social scientist.

Look at our schools and those young students. In these years of independence anniversaries they do not yet have books about themselves, their customs, and histories written by their own people, leave alone in their mother tongues. Robin Hood is no better to a Karamojong pupil than his rugged ancestors; the Masai have better cowboys than those of Texas; *Weep Not Child* is a better explanation of things in the Mau Mau period than the notorious *Uhuru* of Robert Ruark; Shaban's Swahili poems give more warmth than Goethe's German ones to an East African; and Dr. Julius Nyerere brings Shakespeare into the doorsteps of every Swahili speaker by his translation of *Julius Caesar*. We could go on and on, *ad infinitum*, but it will not help; what we want to prove is that we lack cultural and literary foods for consumption; and that this lack is a disadvantage. Now, some of the writings by East Africans should become prescribed school textbooks, just as Achebe's are in Nigeria. James Ngugi's *Weep Not Child* and *The River Between* qualify; in Kenya, *Facing Mount Kenya* could be issued in simplified and abridged forms.

I advocate incorporation of East African writings in the curricula. Our writers are imitators and are yet finding their feet. For that reason I would oppose their pushing away completely the great literary works of the Europeans, Russians, Chinese, Japanese, and Indians, where they are now read. If they are not being read anywhere, I suggest they be introduced. We need to know how our works stand in relation to other contemporary works throughout the world; we also need to compare our works with those by past societies.

These two aims can be realized by studying contemporary literature and types of literature. The latter would put everything in historical perspective.

The Queen's English is as alien as English manners. We need a domestic breed, or rather, crossbreed, full of safari, shamba, jambo, lukiko, rukurato, mwenge, pombe, baisikeli, harambee, uhuru. These words are alive to our ears. India and Ceylon have experienced how difficult it is for a people to choose a national language from many competing ones. But this too I all the yealt. o.k., color etc. which form the insides of English (if he spoke any!) an American English with all the yeah, o.k., color. etc. which form the insides of their Webster dictionaries. A domesticised East African English should be an obedient servant.

Books are counsellors. Where a courtier (or an M.P. or Cabinet Minister for that matter) would be diplomatic or silent, a book, full of wisdom, tried and proved true through the ages, would be the most impartial counsellor.

Writing is a craft. A writer has to be trained the way a carpenter or an architect is trained. A craftsman benefits from training. All those talks about inspiration are nonsense. As I found it epigramatically put somewhere: "inspiration is 99 per cent perspiration." Therefore, if we are to have writers who know their craft or art, we have to go consciously about making them. This is the last point I want to consider in connection with attempting to eradicate our literary poverty. As you will see, it entails the co-operation of various groups.

Our university branches are the best places for spawning our future writers. Ibadan did it, I do not see why Makerere does not. An interested faculty member might inspire individuals directly. *Origin East Africa* is good, as a beginning. It will have more meaning in history if those whose works appear in there become prolific and advanced writers. Courses in the craft of fiction or short story writing or playwriting should be made parts of the English curriculum. (The incorporation of such courses in University English curricula is a common facet of American university catalogues these days. Iowa and Stanford offer writer's workshops in fiction and poetry writing. The success of these courses has been demonstrated by the products of their graduates.)

The Extra-Mural Department of the University of East Africa should conduct seminars and workshops in writing. That department should have a magazine of its own in which the students' efforts would be printed. It could organize East Africa-wide essay, poetry, and fiction competitions, give prizes to winners, and print the winning works in its magazine. This department could also act as the recruiting body recommending promising writers as special students to take courses in our universities in literature and writing whenever these courses are instituted. Scholarship givers should send talented writers to schools where they will better their arts and widen their horizons. The department should continue holding conferences. If they laid emphasis on East Africa, it would have done more profitable work, as far as this writer is concerned, than if it went on collecting all the writers from Africa south of Sahara.

We need writers' clubs. Let's hope that the modest efforts of Ezekiel Mphahlele in Chemchemi Cultural Centre will grow to something big. It is also my hope that Kololo Senior Secondary School's Actors' and Writers' Club flourishes and that other schools follow its example.

That brings me to the uses we are to make of Drama Festivals. Territory-wide festivals could be held so that the secondary schools could present, among other items, one play from outside Africa, one from another part of Africa, and one of its own composition. The last one will lead to originality of composition and production. Prizes for the winning teams could be donated by the East African Literature Bureau or Patel Press, etc. In fact, I do not see the reason why the E.A.L.B. and Patel Press do not have magazines in which to publish writers' works as well advertise their books. They could conduct competitions (I particularly refer to the Patel Press, since E.A.L.B. already organizes literary competitions) for secondary school students, college students, adults, etc. If they did this, they would have done a lot towards fostering writers who would soon be sending them manuscripts.

Our Information Ministries' periodicals for schools should have literary sections devoted to students' writings. We have had enough essay competitions. Fiction and poetry should now be introduced.

We have had radio plays for years. As a new regulation to introduce seriousness and creativity into the works performed, the actors should as a matter of routine, be asked to deposit scripts of their plays with the ministries. If these scripts are well kept in the station's libraries or printed in periodicals, they could be given to future actors. The same goes for T.V.

A writer writes to teach, to entertain, or to exhibit prowess in a medium, or just to release emotion; as such, a writer (or any artist) is decidedly a selfish person — selfish in the sense that he is moved to write from within. If a writer is to write successfully, he must write with all his heart. To write with all his heart, the topic, theme, or problem must be closest to his heart. A writer courts an idea, it accepts him, and then it bosses him. When it has engrossed him he can write with passion. He will write truth — as he conceives it in his mind. To think through a theme, become so obsessed with it that it rules the writer and dictates to him to give it utterance, demands the qualities of an addict, or a faithful servant, or a slave. No wonder there are few people who can submit to the rigours of art. No wonder Coleridge was an opium smoker. No wonder artists go mad — or so we think. No wonder artists have been problem people through the ages: witness the case of Dante. No wonder there is very little difference between the artist and the religious ascetics; between David Thoreau and St. Augustine. The life of a writer —

a dedicated one — is difficult. A writer has to see everything in the world in terms of how they would affect him; if he sees a leprous woman, he has to put himself in her position and see the world through her eyes; if he sees an unfaithful wife he has to know her story very well, even if it takes seven years, in order to be able to relate it in the way Flaubert did *Madame Bovary* and, on the social level, if he sees an injustice done as in the Dreyfus Affair in France, he has to take a personal interest in it like Zola and shout *J'Accuse!*

I do not envy writers and their works. I only wish readers looked through the windows of a writer's kitchen to see how hard the cooking is. Difficult though it is to be a writer, or an artist, there are people marked down for it. They have more sensitivity and passion; they have a more universal outlook towards life and its problems, and they are more readily disposed to volunteer to teach and to entertain, than the average person. No wonder at one time they were supposed to be possessed by muses or stung by the literary bug. These were ways of accounting for the simple fact that once you are destined to be a writer your chance of escape is pretty slim. That gives me hope. I have the hope that our grand-children of folklorists, of fable-tellers still possess that story-telling passion. These are the people who will write stories for us. Let us teach them. Our East African literary barrenness is not everlasting.

Lucy, my wife, had finished cooking supper some hours back. Knowing how wrathful I was when she disturbed my train of thought by talking to me when she came in, she now left me alone to do the task she had set before me, viz. to search for practical ways of removing the literary barrenness of East Africa. When I had finished writing, I took it to her. She was satisfied with the result. Then she asked what I was going to do with these "legislations" — that was her word. I said I would look for a magazine to print it so that more people would read it. She then recommended that I should send it to Ogot's *East Africa Journal,* I told her that I would try. I hoped also that my readers would be concerned as I am. Some of them will be government officials interested in the uplifting of our region culturally; others publishers whose firms are now crying for manuscripts; others private citizens who love entertainment and enlightenment; others schoolboys who yawn over their 'Friends, Romans, and countrymen' or *Paradise Lost;* and others writers sweating through their first manuscripts. From the concerted efforts of all these will come our text-books, poems, essays, short stories, novels, and plays.

You see, our literary discussion group composed of Nigerians, Ghanians, Sierra Leonians, South Africans and Francophones merely adjourned today when I was humiliated by East Africa's literary barrenness. Tomorrow I expect to receive the secretary's circular informing us about the next place and time of meeting. I am not going there again until seven novels, seven volumes of poems, seven biographies, seven plays, and twenty-seven social science works have been produced by East Africans. Yet if I do not go, my wife will trouble me no end; she does not want a coward for a husband. But if I go, my virago of a muse will torment me till I write another lament. But then I would have to box my head more times and squeeze it tighter between my large hands. Doctors tell me that if I press my head too much, it becomes mis-shapen, and I grow war-like like the fighting, jumping Watutsi. I prefer some sanity. Please, keep me sane. You can do this by writing. Each East African who writes increases the number of works I want to carry with me to that meeting.

After all, why should Nigerians have more writers? We have a greater land (and water) area than they. If the idea of a competition frightens you to death, at least do something to get me out of my dilemma. I have a virago wife who henpecks me if I do not go to the literary meeting, and a virago of a muse who torments me each time I think of East Africa's literary barrenness.

Tibble, Tutuola, Taban, and Thugs

Dear reader, imagine an English lady. She is elderly, a school mistress to boot, a spinster as well, of a rather phlegmatic character, dressed mostly in dimiti. She is also the centre of gossip to a group of other elderly ladies. She is a little feeble-minded, timid and circumlocutionary, given to repeating herself, and would traverse the flat, boggy, English moor in many directions before picking up courage to go to the drug store to buy tissues. Imagine such a lady lifted straight out of a Henry James's novel, carrying a handbag (with tissues in it for touching her nose whenever the journey on the moor (a surface journey without much knowledge of what lies underneath) gets tougher or the wind gives her hay fever). She is toting a satchel with her other hand. With this satchel, she has gone in and out, in and out, in and out... of bookstores and libraries (mostly libraries).

Then one day, you meet her right in the door of the library. Perhaps she knocks against you. In a piercing voice she cries out, "Excuse me!" and you murmur: "Sure." But suddenly she does not leave the gate for you. You are being observed. Is it because you are an African? Yes. But why that look? The lady is interested. She wants to know you. She wants to invite you to her home. She writes your name down in her note book (small, neat handwriting in black ink).

You get interested (you are a male and perhaps you are married). But she is not so young. You begin to wonder what the lady wants to do with you. She spares you more perplexity. The lady is a writer. She is writing a critical survey of African literature to be called *African-English Literature: A Short Survey and Anthology of Prose and Poetry up to 1965*. And her name is Miss Anne Tibble. "Would you like to come to tea please?" "Why, yes," (with eagerness). "Next Saturday, and with my friends." "Why, yes," (with disappointment).

Saturday came. You went: teeth brushed, shoes polished, body washed, arm pits deodorized, hair well brushed. And punctual, too. Her group is already there, waiting for you: elderly ladies, perhaps working for charity organizations including Race Relations, an ex-missionary or two; refined school teachers, widows, two straight-backed men propelled by their tottering buxom wives; two of her own students (for she is a teacher, teaching in one of the cheap new colleges planted in the English villages). One of the students present is an African student in her school. He says nothing of consequence. Perhaps he is well-behaved. Maybe he has no opinion and therefore expresses none.

Tea is brought in. And a famous cake which had already survived two previous slaughters, makes its presence on the table felt. You sense it: the atmosphere changes. One elderly lady to your left gives you a look which intimates that you will be banished to Australia if you dare eat a lot of this dear cake. Everybody is agreed the cake must live. The cake pleads in all its pores:

"Please, don't eat me all. My mistress wants me to serve her next week end".

Miss Tibble asks you if you need some more. You shake your head. She insists. You resist. Another member of the group urges you to have a little more. But the cake gives you a harder and meaner look. You say, "No, I am satisfied..." (with only a bite).

Somehow or other, African literature crops up as a topic for discussion. Perhaps one of the 'girls' dragged it in, perhaps Miss Tibble herself introduced it, you can't remember. What you remember very well is that all of a sudden Miss Tibble brightened up (very unlike the cake-serving one of a few minutes back). Her grey woollen suit seems to fit her well. She is in the limelight.

As the discussion progresses, you begin to sense that the other people were already familiar with the major points. For, when one began a sentence on Achebe, another completed it, with general approval. More could have been said on Tutuola, but there seemed to be a taboo about it. The name Dostoyevsky came up obscurely once and disappeared just as obscurely. Chivalry came up and the straight backed gentlemen (one of whom went by the name of Stabler) ,were rejuvenated, much to the delight of the 'girls'.

Your time is up. You have to go to read your History of the British Empire. Miss Tibble promises you an autographed copy of her *African-English Literature* as soon as it comes out of October House Inc. On the way to your digs you revolve over in your mind whether the credit for the book should go to Miss Tibble alone or she has to share it with her cronies. You are more inclined to honour the tea-party group. You also conclude that blames for faults in the famous book will have to be shared by all Tibbles. (Her group was the major audience she had in mind.)

*   *   *

True to her promise, Miss Tibble sends you a copy of *African-English Literature*. Eagerly, you flap over the pages. As sure as things could be, Dame Elspeth Huxley has been dragged in to warn everybody that a person of another culture cannot write very well on another culture. Wonderful. (But the Dame herself carries the incongruous title of African Correspondent for William Buckley's conservative magazine, *The National Review*, and writes rather conservative articles on African Kabakas, herself and Rhodesia.)

Judith Gleason (another woman, this time American) has already prejudiced Miss Tibble against Tutuola. Hence, you are reminded that "Tutuola is not a novelist." What is he? you wonder. The English moor and bog present themselves straight away with Miss Tibble endlessly wandering there like a witch who has lost her broom.

Then, what other name is there? Why, Mphahlele, of course. His footsteps are discernible all over the moor. You shake your head and say: "Zeke, if you keep on wandering all over the world, you won't write a novel. Shut yourself up in the castle of your skin and write."

Dostoyevsky's bones have been exhumed to testify that Okolo is his grandson. (What is a broomstick for if it can't dig up a Russian grave? What is it for if it can't fly safely over fighting Nigeria? The witch achieves a space feet of joining dead Dostoyevsky and Okolo (dead?) by it.)

46

But she has problems with her vocabulary. Some technical words seem to be outside the ken of the tea-party group.

Yet Miss Tibble is strong in Relativity. Relativity of the comparativity and Universality of cultural things. The comparison of things 'those' people there do like 'us' are strewn all over the moor, like the bristles of a broom poorly tied. It would have been good public relationship work were it not also patronizing to Africans.

Sometimes you wonder whether she is saying Africans and children are one thing and elders and Europeans are synonymous. Especially when she is confronted by the Protean Tutuola. (She becomes a female proteus herself and is so shifty in the vast moor, it takes all one's efforts to pin her down!)

She is also a diplomat. Very careful not to offend the African gods that matter.

A spinster herself, our heroine has love for romances, gallantry, and female view points. (Research by an American foundation has revealed that teen-agers and spinsters are the greatest consumers of romances. Teenagers: in order to know how to go about it. Spinsters: to have a peep at what the lucky ones are doing and to enjoy it by proxy. N.B. This research took a longer time than the Kinsey Report and is estimated to have cost over $7,000,000.)

Miss Tibble dreams of riding a camel in the Sudanese desert beside a gallant Shukria ("they are like us"). Before she changes her moor for the desert, it would be in her best interest to make peace first with Dayan. One-eyed generals can't be fooled, cf. Nelson. They have simple vision: no paralex.

* * *

Let's move closer to Miss Tibble. (Our imagined "Miss Tibble" you understand.) And engage in a running commentary.

Page XI: "No person of one race and culture can truly interpret from the angle of individuals belonging to a totally different race and culture." — Elspeth Huxley: *Red Strangers.*

Having barricaded herself with this quotation, she (Miss Tibble) then forgets most western literature and criticism and plunges deep in the dark African jungle.

(No point. Your being a stranger is taken for granted. What is needed is exactly nothing less than an interpretation from that "totally different race and culture" — and a consciously different interpretation — of this thoroughly human drama being acted out and recorded in 'that' culture. No dog goes into a manger with the eyes of a horse. Where there are differences, one ought to acknowledge them when one is establishing a *modus vivendi*. No communist critic becomes a capitalist first in order to criticize a thoroughly bourgeois novel. By the same token, the Roman Catholic Church would not have its long list of proscribed books if the censors saw with the writers' eyes.)

Page XV: "Africans assessing African writing and African problems have been quoted whenever possible. But happily from more than one point of view — there is African creative work in plenty compared with the amount of African criticism yet. Chary of European approaches to African work, African critics as well as writers are still groping for their own terms and perspectives. Some people might say that African literature is still searching for its own definitions. And so, of course, it is; and it will continue to search."

(. . .African economics is still searching for its own definitions. And so, of course, it is; and it will continue to 'search.' . . . So. . . So what? Nothing. . . except that critics of literature are critics of literature just as trainers for Olympic games are trainers for Olympic games, and makers of bombs are makers of bombs. In short, a first rate European critic of European literature can be a first rate critic of African literature *qua* literature. Dryden criticized English literature according to French tenets, and he did a good job too. D. H. Lawrence was quite insightful about certain American classics. And no Americans have beaten De Toqueville and Myrdal. Sometimes the 'in' people are hypnotized and only foreigners can break the spell. If you Europeans and Americans are shy or easily put off we bold Africans will plunge into the depth of Albion herself and heat things up vigorously.)

Page 28. "Yet it is English, its poets, Whitman, Frost, Wilbur, and Creeley, astonishingly so."

(Lady, your slips are showing! Mend it. Plug the holes with full stops.)

Page 29. " 'Heathen' is another word that denigrates and so misunderstands."

('Heathen' must really be a live member of our species to be able to 'misunderstand.')

Page 34. ". . .he who has no shadow. . .means. . . a man who isn't strong enough, either physically or in personality, for the sun to cast his shadow on the ground."

("He who has no shadow" simply means "He is so inconsequential he lacks even a ghost!" Whenever you are frightened doesn't your heart rush to your mouth and your ghost jets out through another aperture?)

Page 34: "As Okot p' Bitek points out — human societies are now seen by ethnologists as 'functional';

African society and people are not 'simple'. European society has not evolved from the 'simple' to the civilized. Both African and Europeans are complex. Terms such as 'primitive', 'savage', and 'simple', p' Bitek observes, are therefore now used only by 'die-hard intellectual conservatives.' "

(Yes, madam, Africans are not 'simple' — but aren't they 'savage' and strong?)

(Malinowski's school of anthropology. I agree that cultures are 'functional', (for what else could they be?) . But this is a mere description of a manifestation. Ethnologists may spend their time watching cultures in action, bearing witness to an act in progress. But they ought to add depth to their operations by searching out the roots from which these 'functionings' arose. They ought to explore the bottoms of cultures and trace out the path the germs took in coming to the surface where they are now seen as 'functionings.' For surely cultures originated somewhere and sometime (barring divine inspiration) , and they developed and changed from month to month, year to year, they evolved through the ages through rough and calm .To say that water flows in the river is to say the obvious. One ought to explore the growth of a river from the youthful stage when water comes in a torrent and tears grass, trees, earth apart, to the middle age when it has steadied, and old age when it has reached a stage of quietude and rarely moves. There can be a difference of opinion in determining when the 'savage' stage begins and when it ends, and whether it should be called 'savage' or 'youthful' or 'ravaging'. These arguments can be very hot. But there cannot be any question about evolution whatsoever. It looks to me as if Professor Malinowski (and his group) committed an intellectual fraud (wittingly or unwittingly) and corrupted science in order to humour his friends from the savage and barbarian cultures.)

Page 35: 'Onlookers will see throughout the discussion the one wide issue both direct and indirect that concerns African writers deeply but also concerns writers everywhere."

(We need a comma after 'the one wide' issue, and 'indirect'.)

(In literature, there cannot be an 'onlooker'. Everybody ought to be involved, and involved totally and deeply. When I read Oliver Twist, I experienced hunger: hunger neither English nor African, but simple human hunger. When I toured Europe I saw the spires, I saw massive crosses and other symbols in front and inside the churches. These cried out for my spiritual responses, stimulated me, and I gave of whatever piety I had. (In Saint Peter's Cathedral, there is an iron statue of St. Peter. Women from everywhere were active kissing St. Peter's toe. The toe is so worn out that I think by the year 2000 St. Peter will not have even half an inch of a toe left.) It has also been reported that Hottentots danced when Bach was played to them the first time. One must be a monster to remain an 'onlooker' when so human, so pervasive, so universal a thing as art (beauty) is being discussed.)

Page 43: "The back of the minds of his (Solomon T. Plaatje's) Barolongs, Matabeles, and Zulus, on life's principle of almost infinite variety within essential likeness, are curiously similar to the backs of European minds."

(Comparatively. You came very close to seeing light but most of the time retreated into shade. How can such a bold truth be reconciled to your circumspection fore and after? Isn't a European critic at home in this atmosphere, and therefore free to express his "curiously similar" views?

(Statements like 'Are of any culture', 'could be found in any culture' abound. And Miss Tibble, within limits, analyses plots, and gives us comparisons of one work to another (not very many, these.) But she does not go deep, does not seriously criticise, has very little light of her own for illuminating a work from within. Now, let's go to love.)

Page 77: Dobeit 6: Love.

"Come El Wagel, my camel to her who has our own nature; her slender throat high between ear and shoulder, her heavy-hung hair needs no false hair to lengthen. In love she will have me, for no man is bolder." (And no woman either!)

(But let's permit Miss Tibble to speak.)

Page 77: "Now let us look at what the singer of the sixth dobeit (Shukria (Sudan) poem) has found in the girl of his choice: first of all she is like him; she thinks as he does, they will, therefore, agree; she will not thwart him secretly. Second, she has two beauties that are important — a high, slender throat (we may recall how Annie Laurie's neck was 'like the swan's'), and thick, rich hair. Thick, rich hair on a woman's head is a token, a symbol, of faithful womanhood and of passion, ... his love's passion might triumphantly match the singer's boldness."

(Comment: No Comment!
Let's go for more gallantry.)
Page 77: Dobeit 7, Love (2)
"I swam the White Nile, the *arak* savannah crossed:
Sword ready, the saddle on my camel tossed.
What can death matter? Life is never lost:

Have I not kissed her lips whose cheeks are scar embossed?

(Comment: Supply your own.)

Page 89: "There is probably a strong likeness between classical Greek society and Nigerian traditional society, and John Pepper Clark is exploring this."

(For Greek the word is 'classical'; for Nigeria, the synonym is 'traditional.')

(Yes and No. There may be a strong likeness in Greek 'traditional' and Nigerian 'traditional' cultures and John Pepper Clark is trying to explore this. There may also be no likeness (in so far as we can talk about 'likeness' and 'unlikeness' in cultures) and John Pepper Clark is simply adopting Greek technique for use on a work in hand. There is no harm in that. In fact, we need more Greek, English, etc., ways of doing things adopted by Africans. We can't allow you to monopolize the ways. It is ridiculous to bar an African from adopting foreign techniques. If these techniques work in, say, Rome, they should work elsewhere too. It is not so much the technique as the personal style the artist has, his personal mark with which he stamps his works which is important. Homer wrote *The Odyssey* in a Greek and Homerian way; Virgil wrote the same story in his *Aeneid* in a thoroughly Roman and Virgilian way. That rake Ovid covered episodes of that war in a throughly amorous Ovidian way. What Racine and Corneille dramatised were Renaissance French life transposed in ages and places past and transmitted through the forge of these disparate writers. Peter Weiss's *Marat/Sade* is thoroughly Jewish, German Nazism, as well as being thoroughly Peter Weiss. The historical Marat de Sade is merely used as a figure of speech and a vehicle for thought.

(Apart from the particular cultural outlook one gives to one's work, there is the individual philosophy of the author, his objects of values; his way of exposition, his use of language. So any African could write a Chinese drama and yet it would be African as well, branded with his personal seal. With things like the novel, plays, epic poetry, Noh theatre, Chinese landscape painting, the African artist has to go to school to acquire them. Unless he wants to remain circumscribed in his poor culture, he simply has to learn them in order to enrich his culture, as well as his intellectual outlook and repertoire, increase his perception and sensitivity and reaction.)

Page 92: "The theme of *The Voice* suggests the motif treated at far greater length in Dostoyevsky's *The Idiot.*"

(At least we now have an African writer comparable to Dostoyevsky in major aspects. Bravo for the writer. Double Bravo for the finder (discoverer, inventor?). Perhaps... perhaps... maybe... we dimwitted ones should have our eyes opened, so that we may perceive this glaring truth which had eluded us.)

(Miss Tibble, what exactly is the 'theme' of *The Voice*? We know (you have told us) that it 'suggests' something, but first of all tell us what the theme is and trust our slow minds to examine slowly whether that famous 'theme' really 'suggests' ... The theme ... suggests the motif — what is this 'motif' so 'suggested' by the 'theme'? Cf. the horn of the bull suggests the neck of the swan which also suggests the scales of the snake.)

(In expository writing one can't hide behind unknown quantities to describe other unknown quantities. Too bad 'theme' and 'motif' are not English words. Miss Tibble would have known them. For, Sirs, Madams, 'theme', 'motif', 'quantum', 'psychedelic' are technical words. We can excuse an English woman's ignorance of them. (Moreover, they are not in any way connected with broom flight!)

Page 94: "Dylan Thomas rightly hailed *The Palm-Wine Drinkard* as 'thronged, grisly', a 'tall devilish story'."

(And he hailed it wrongly. 'Thronged' — yes (like a bunch of grapes!), 'grisly', yes (like a monster's tail!), 'tall' — (like a pillar, yes!), otherwise no. No. No. No. Perhaps Tutuola's (no, not Tutuola's problems) critic's problems all began with Dylan Thomas.)

(But Dylan Thomas read the Pre-socratics too: Pythagoreanism: From the *Golden Verses,* Lines 71-72:

("When after divesting yourself of your mental body you arrive in the pure upper aether, you will be a god, and immortal, incorruptible; *and death shall have no dominion over you."*

(Dylan Thomas: 'And Death Shall Have no Dominion.'

(title of poem and refrain) :

'And death shall have no dominion.
Dead men naked they shall be one
With the man in the *wind* and the west moon.
When their bones are picked clean bones gone,
They shall have stars at elbow foot.' (emphasis added)

This is our scholar poet who also read Hesiod and Homer (we assume) but who could not see the Hesiodic, the Homeric, the mythical in Tutuola's work. He showers epithets previously reserved for rare, exotic Arabic writings with sensationalism on this *sui generis* (!) work. Either *The Odyssey* is equally 'thronged grisly,' 'tall, devilish story', or *The Palm-Wine Drinkard* is classical,

5*

ancient, and great. Equal praise for equal work, or equal blame for equal work.)

Page 96: "After such wide-of-the-mark praise of his first book, Tutuola has had to suffer an unfair backlash of dispraise of his later books."

(Miss Tibble, do you mean Tutuola was over-praised? Overpraised for the wrong reasons? Does not deserve the praises? What were the causes of the later 'dispraise'? To cut him down to size? To efface a wrong already committed — an act of revenge? Or just strict adherence to normal critical attitudes? Take a stand.)

Page 96: "... (the) terrible 'half-child' Zurrjir, who emerges from the Drinkard's wife's swollen *left* thumb."

(There is a left-handed deal; Jesus sits on the right hand of God; Zeus bore a child through his head, one came from his thigh.)

Page 97: "... this horror talks 'with a lower voice like a telephone'."

(Tutuola's dramatic way of saying that the thing was really a ghost. (Any ingenious director of Hamlet is advised henceforward to take cue from Tutuola. The Ghost of Hamlet's dead father talked with a 'lower voice like a telephone'.) Ghosts never shout. There's no chill in that.)

Page 99: "... child-like lack of sophistication."

(Where is the 'childlikeness' and the 'lack of sophistication'?)

Page: "This non-sophistication could not fail to captivate many European readers."

(If they were captivated by that, and only that, they may go and hunt the Loch Ness Monster. I thought some of them knew something 'grisly' and 'thronged' on the surface, but knew it was also quite deep, as deep as one's proboscis can fathom. In any case, Eric Fromm's book

Forgotten Language is recommended to them as an introduction.)

Page 99: " (Tutuola) is ...lovable...lovable (sic!) ; often unintentionally, funny; as when the Drinkard thanks God 'that He had created me without beauty'."

Let the military dictators in Greece burn all Greek art and writings, let the world cast all Greek words into the sea or burn them with napalm or send them to Venus, but let us have Book Three of *The Iliad* and we can reconstruct Greek culture. The essences of Greek are to be found in *The Iliad* Book Three.

(Beauty — Love — Lust: all three going together;

(Brain-over-Brawn;

(Fidelity;

(Respect for Gods and Elders;

(Sticking by one's fellow citizens through thick and thin;

(Culture over everything else:

All heroes without intellect died: Hector, Achilles, Ajax; *those with winning tongues lived*: Odysseus, Paris (it is he who just seduced Helen with his sweet talks and looks; it was also he (the coward, of all the people) who shot the arrow which killed valiant, wrathful, Achilles in the fatal heel) ; Beauty and Culture was 'kidnapped' from Achaia, taken to Troy, and later returned to Achaia, still loved, like a museum piece (in the personification of Helen) .

Helen, the paragon of beauty, the epigony of the highest cultural values held in great esteem by Trojans and Achaians, is the object of competition. Achaians produced her, nourished her. The most civilized cultured Trojan, Paris, came and kidnapped the cultural essence of Achaia.

The Trojans are 'breakers of horses', they live in the land where the 'soil is rich'. They are, therefore, 'farmers, agronomists', villagers! The Achaians, on the other hand, live in the 'land of fair women', are 'bronze-armoured'. They are artists. (Read Homer's description of the display of artistry on the shield of Achilles.)

The ideal togetherness of citizens is given us:

"But the Achaian men went silently, breathing valor,

"Stubbornly minded each in his heart to stand by the others."

Respect for Nestorianism is given us:

"Always it is, that the hearts in the younger men are frivolous,

"but when an elder man is among them, he looks behind him,

"and in front, so that all comes out far better for both sides."

Paris (Alexandros) challenged Menelaos to a single combat, but later chickened out.

But Hektor (brute force who did not understand culture) saw him and in words of shame rebuked him:

"Evil Paris, beautiful, woman-crazy, cajoling,

better you never been born or killed unwedded.

Truly I could have wished it so; it would be far better than to have you with us to our shame, for others to sneer at.

Surely now the flowing-haired Achaians laugh at us, thinking you are our bravest champion, only because your

looks are handsome, but there is no strength in your heart, no courage."

Alexandros acknowledges Hektor's martial spirit —
but cautioned:

"...yet do not bring up against me the sweet favours
of golden Aphrodite.

"Never to be cast away are the gifts of the gods,
magnificent,

"which they give of their own will, no man could
have them for wanting them."

Helen and Paris are the darlings of the gods and
goddesses of culture. Helen walks through fire and never
gets burnt.

Paris who knew truth (truth is beauty, beauty
truth), as soon as he had escaped death from Menelao's
spear and sword, runs straight home. He orders that Helen
come to him.

"Come, then ...let us go to bed, turn to love-making.

"Never before as now has passion enmeshed my
passion" — a logically sound psychological sequel.

Priam is discussing Odysseus with Helen, "the
daughter descended of Zeus". She points out Odysseus
to the King:

"This one is Laertes' son, resourceful Odysseus,
    who grew up in the country, rough thought it be, of
        Ithaka,
to know every manner of shiftiness and crafty counsels."
Odysseus is a presophist. He goes through hell, cave,
straits, by applying his 'shiftiness' and 'craftiness' and
comes out alive.

Trojan elders — too old to fight, sit watching the
young bloods, from the ramparts. They pass mature
observations:

"And these, as they saw Helen along the tower
    approaching
murmuring softly to each other uttered their winged
    words:
'Surely there is no blame on Trojans and strong-
    greaved Achaians
if for long time they suffer hardship for a woman like
    this one.
Terrible is the likeness of her face to immortal
    goddesses.
Still, though she be such, let her go away in the
    ships, lest
she be left behind, a grief to us and our children.' "

Psychologically, the Trojans have already lost the
war for culture. Read those two last lines again.

Was there any 'real' Trojan War? Hardly. The whole
thing is a parable. Written after the events. A
reconstruction of what the Greeks thought to have
occurred in the past. An explanation for manifest
phenomena. In a word, the Trojan War was a war of
Adjectives, Proper Nouns and Abstract Nouns.

The Trojan War is a 'tall story', told to embody
the things that Achaians and Trojans held most dearly in
morals, art, philosophy, etc. So are the stories of Amos
Tutuola. The journeys are clothes lines for displaying
values. The Greeks and Trojans slaughtered each other
for the sake of Beauty. Tutuola's Yoruba hero knows
full well the woes beauty brings. In one sentence he
denigrates Greek civilization: "Thank God, I was
created without beauty."

It is Wisdom, and Wealth obtained through
adventures by a resourceful man who has inborn faith
in his own abilities, those of his juju, and in God, the

Yoruba valued most. Tutuola's works and those of Chief Fagunwa give us that impression.)

Page 99: "Faithful Mother (provided) a special room in her White Tree for her guests to 'play gamble'!"

(Life is a gamble; any adventurer is a gambler; any writer is a gambler; Columbus was a gambler; Schramme and his mercenaries and Tshombe were gamblers; Pascal was a gambler (his calculus was the child of gambling.))

Page 99: "The Drinkard and his wife sold their *deaths* but kept their *fears*."

(Without fear, death has no dominion, meaning, pang. Read what Kierkegaard says about fear and trembling in order to find the context of the Tutuolan fragment.)

Page 100: "Simbi's 'voice' could wake the deads".

(There's Black Orpheus for you.)

Page 100: Simbi's girl companions are: "Rali, Sala, Kadara": Hunger, Poverty, Punishment. They leave her to go to Multi-Coloured people.

(There was a prince once called Gautama Buddha. He was riding on a chariot one day. He asked the chariot driver what thing existed beyond the horizon. The chariot driver did not wish to disturb the equanimity of the beloved prince so he said: Nothing. Buddha ordered that he be driven to see Nothing. Prince and chariot driver went and lo, what did they find but Rali, Sala, and Kadara. From that moment Buddha started the First Cultural Revolution.

'Multi-Coloured People' are simply people 'jaded' as to character, morals, philosophy.)

Page 101: "...all five (books) are fine fairy tales as well as contriving to be something more, for boys and girls and grown-ups."

(Miss Tibble, make up your mind. If you think they are fairy tales, say so. If you are sure they 'contrive to be something more' exercise your mind more and give us one or two of those things they 'contrive' to be.

Tutuola is our first philosopher. There's no doubt about that. Myths are man's first philosophies. And, upon myths, all later philosophies and arts and cultures arise. Recorders of myths are writers of philosophy text books. In his medium is the message.

The disparagers of Tutuola are all barbarians, Turks, Hottentots; or Ostrogoths, black fellows, infidels; in other words: Vandals, pigmies, Angles; also known as Tartars, Visigoths, Gauls; sometimes called: tribesmen, Gentiles, Maoris, Saxons; otherwise named: Trojans, witches, Groats; in a word: uncultured.)

*　　*　　*

Miss Tibble, (our imaginary Miss Tibble) isn't it rather late now for you to engage in proving that we are men also? Where were you when we were out in the 'cauld blast' being tossed left and right by missionaries, traders, empire builders? Probably attending the meetings of the Royal Society for the Prevention of Cruelty to Animals, at the time when the 'humanity' of dogs and cats and rats was already proved beyond doubt. Isn't a helper, my Dear Lady, a one who gives the drowning man the rope when he has already pulled himself out of the torrent?

Keep your atonement to yourself now. Convert it into ready cash, acceptable everywhere as a means of exchange, stronger than the British pound, more honoured than the British Passport. It is now for each person to find out the most durable cash he should use.

We can stand telling remarks. But we'll never forgive those who humour us. The discovery that one had been made happy falsely makes one sick; makes one want to vomit out all that dog's meat one had been fed with disguised as mutton. If you want to be my friend, tell me to my face what you honestly feel about me.

It is folly to imagine that an African, any African, is the best critic of things African. Few English people are experts on English language, or on Shakespeare. Whoever wants to excel in something has to apply himself with industry and diligence and for a length of time. A Papuan can become an expert Swahili grammarian just as a Zanzibari can, so long as they study hard. Senghor is reputed one of the foremost French grammarians. At this early stage of African literary criticism, do we have any ground for grudging Ulli Beier, Gerald Moore, Janheinz Jahn, Madame Kesteloot — on top of Ezekiel Mphahlele — the titles of 'the foremost critics' of African literature? If the list has few African names, isn't it a challenge for Africans to try harder? It is the height of folly for Africans to declare that African culture or literature is the one branch of knowledge beyond the attainment of all non- Africans. Which African knows more about Africa's past than, say, Dr. Leakey?

*　　*　　*

There is nobody I fear more than the Africanist, or the mercenary, or the prostitute.

Especially the American Africanist. In the Social Sciences, America has never had half-a-dozen idealist, integrity-filled, conscientious people. Morgan stands out above everybody else in the beginning of Social Science. C. Wright Mills beats the moderns in both the scope and importance of his researches and his attempt (unsuccessful) to give the social scientists ethics and a respectability. The prostituted social scientists of course include the subgroup Africanists. Here, we have the man Melville Herskovits who fought and lost the war of trying to keep politics (espionage, sabotage, etc.) out of the social sciences. He is the only scholar (in the traditional sense of the word) among the Africanists. All the others decided American nationalism came above everything else; grants for universities should be secured under all pretexts; foreign travels are more attractive than pure scholarship; and that so long as you can be paid for it, any research or paper or project will be undertaken. I wish Melville were alive when C.I.A. involvement in academia was revealed.

Projects Camelot are being undertaken under various disguises. Scholars (?) and professionals (?) who travel to foreign countries are asked to be interviewed by the C.I.A. first and are given assignments to do on the side. And why not? The money is there. Besides, the superiority of the West has to be maintained at all costs, as Margaret Mead and other leading cyberneticians advocate.

As a member of the Third World, I was really worried about our fate. And then, Newark happened. And then Detroit happened. And Wisconsin University. I sighed with relief. If these instruments, developed by social scientists and technocrats are effective, they will be used on us; they will also be used on American citizens in America whenever similar conditions arise. Thank you very much, Americans, for developing methods for controlling peoples in the Third World. In the era of national expansion, you point the bullets at us. In the age of national contractions you will use those same bullets on American Negroes, American students, American businessmen, American common men, American labourers,

American intellectuals, American generals, American presidents.

So, as I said, thank you very much.

You hear loud shouts about population explosion now. Nobody is complaining about population increase *qua* population increase. In America, it so happened that high (wealthy) class values favour the maintenance of a very small family. Middle class America has what it calls an 'ideal' family of around five people. So the only people who 'populate' the country, the streets, the ghettoes, are poor whites and Negroes. And they live on relief (money), and they strike and demand, and they riot. So, they are a menace to 'society.' They are to be controlled (law and order will be maintained). They are to be told to stop 'populating'.

The Third World pesters America for aid and food. (There is food in plenty in the world, and in the United States. But the food is in the wrong hands.) So, tell them to plan better. And tell them to 'populate' less. Tell Indians to sterilize themselves, like rams for sale so that they fuck and beget not.

The Third World is not all that friendly. China (and all the Third World) breeds red peril, pestilence. So, establish organizations, support organizations, which will convince these enemies in this state of war to cut down on the number of Viet Congs they are breeding. Develop chemicals with which you can conduct the biogical war, with which you can pollute streams, atmosphere, plants, food stuffs, and make the enemies imbeciles, dwarfs, nonentities.

So, thank you again, thorough Americans. But there is no guarantee that an American administration pressed to the 'sticking point' will not avail itself of these tools on its American 'enemies'. 1984 in the advanced countries first? Or after? After. First.

* * *

Where does African literature come in? Literature is one of the means of social control. So, if Africans establish fixed, rigid boxes around themselves as the Negritudists would wish, or the African 'nonsensists' viz.: Socialism, Personality, etc., we shall have made it that easier for our governments (lackeys) to control us for their sake and that of their controllers. For that matter, African thinkers, writers, must become visionaries; must understand implications of present events; must extrapolate the course of these events into the future. This is the time to establish the traditions of the future. (Thank God our traditions have been destroyed for us, we don't have to fight a Cultural Revolution). So approve when you see the reason for approval. Oppose very vigorously (they won't allow themselves to be used by the manipulators if they know that we shall hang them for it) when you see the reason for opposition.

Traditional African Literature

How to control a community and the individuals who compose it is a difficult problem; it has occupied man since he became a social animal. Different methods have been used, all of them reducible to these two: that which deposits power in a small body which controls the masses; and that which inculcates beliefs in the individual and then expects him to live by the beliefs. This latter is possibly the product of the former. The small body of rulers is made up of a select group whose claim to leadership might be bravery, intellectual superiority, or heredity. Since this group cannot obviously supervise the activities of the numerous followers for all the twenty-four hours of the day, it usually appoints subordinates. But the task is still too much even for the rulers and their subordinates. Hence the invention of beliefs, laws, myths, traditions — all types of sanctions and regulations — which the members absorb through life-long acculturation and which guide their activities through life. If the acculturation is successful, there is no need for the constant presence of the rulers to have things done or not done. In such a case, each individual's mind becomes a storehouse of commandments labelled 'do' and 'don't'. These, in ideal situations, are comparable to iron-filings at rest. An infraction of the 'don't' disturbs the actor's mind and whole constitution just as much as passing a magnet over iron-filings. The mind therefore craves for equanimity, a state of well-being, with the result that the individual tends to become a conformist. It is when the individual has accepted all the sanctions of his community and is guided in the performance of his daily business by them that we say he has a conscience. That is the ultimate stage in group control.

The chief purpose of traditional African literature was the formation of a group conscience. The beliefs, myths, legends, proverbs, folklores, fables, riddles, conundrums were instruments fashioned by the clans or tribes for the inculcations of standards of action and philosophies of life which reflect the tribe's history and general character. From the testimonies of the learned, and our elders, about the lack of morals and disruption of society after the introduction of western culture into Africa, we may conclude that the traditional methods of cohesion were very successful. There was a very high degree of group consensus — on any idea or course of action. The wonder about it all is that it was by word of mouth that this culture was transmitted, a testimony to the superiority of oral over written methods of teaching. For, through 'spoken literature' Africans have been very successful in imparting culture from generation to generation.

The chief purposes of African literature are two: to teach culture to the children or stranger and to teach wisdom. It is difficult to learn any new knowledge. As such, our 'teachers', cognizant of that fact, devised entertaining stories for the presentation of certain facts and truths of life. Many commentators, both African and non-African, have mistakenly held that that was the sole purpose of

African oral literature. The entertainment is merely the means of attaining the end, which is the imparting of knowledge. Moreover some of these stories might have been actual satires on the contemporaries of the story composers, it behoved the narrators to call John, 'Rabbit' and Mary, 'Duyker', in order to avoid quarrels for slander, or creations of ill-feelings. Children, for whom the stories were told, are more disposed to attend, to learn, and to remember the funny, humorous, and grotesque.

A good story told well is good for the body and the mind. The contents of the story evoke certain emotions in the hearers which lead to the catharsis of Aristotle. Audience participation in singing choruses from the songs with mimicking or miming, and dramatizing parts of the story incite hearty responses and provide wholesome exercises. Since each listener is expected to tell a story also, it pays to be alert in order to comprehend and retain all stories for future evening sessions.

African spoken literature is composed of pure prose, pure poetry, and a mixture of prose and poetry. The prose, divisible into fiction and non-fiction, not only deals with social codes, rituals, taboos, proverbs, riddles, stories of deities, but also with the histories of human origin, the legends of the tribe, the myths which accumulated through the ages, and other phenomena and noumena that have been the preoccupation of the tribe. All of these are recollections and reinterpretations of past 'events' recounting human encounters with the vicissitudes of life, explanations of cosmogony, cosmology, and all aetiological exercises.

Proverbs are epigrammatic; they are the summations of wisdom, ethics, morals, and values; they are founded on actual or imaginary (but probable) experiences. Their brevity makes them handy tools to be carried about and made use of under various circumstances. You may remember a proverb or you may not. If you do not you will regret it. But with taboo it is different; what is taboo is taboo. If you break a taboo you may have sinned against man, or spirit, or deity. The only way by which you can reconcile yourself with the offended party is by the performance of a ceremony. Puns and tongue-twisters sharpen the wits. The knowledge of the long names which are usually sung as forms of address saves him the embarrassment which follows inappropriate addressing of the dignitaries, one's elders and relatives.

Tales that moralize form the bulk of fiction. Most of them are humorously told trickster tales. Although animal protagonists outnumber human ones to a great degree, these tales were developed wholly and essentially in human societies; animals are used as a technical device. These animal protagonists may be regarded as cultural 'heroes'. The cultural heroes of one tribe have their counterparts in another tribe. The choice of the particular animals as protagonists and minor characters is dependent very much on geographical factors of fauna and flora distribution. There are numbers of tales which revolve around particular themes. Hence we can speak of them as 'cycles'. There are cycles of demon lovers, and ingratitude, etc.

All tales were 'composed' long ago; exactly when they were formed cannot be said. Although it is possible that new ones have come into being it was not the common thing. The narrators had the same relationship to the stories as pianists and other musicians have to composition before them: skilful rendition or interpretation. They could also make variations. These stories are long; they are the longest form of spoken literature, after (if we include among them) the heroic chants. However long a tale may be, it is merely an elaborate way of illustrating an epigram, proverb, or 'law' of life or nature. The lesson is a concise statement usually appended to the end of the story. In a sense we can say that a tale is built backwards: from the moral at the end, through the 'body' and right up to the 'beginning'. All these tales assume that man and nature, man and spirit, man and man, are always in a state of well-being. They continue so till man (or the animal character representing him) transgresses. Then there is chaos. Retribution is visited upon the head of the transgressor and the tribe just as a thing of joy would have been shared by the whole community. The offender and his community take steps to purify himself and reconcile him with the offended party. According to this outlook towards life, there was no chance happening, no happening, that is, which could not be explained in terms of conflicts between the individual and the forces I have mentioned above. Your own offence, the machinations of evil neighbours, the anger of ancestral and nature spirits were all causes of suffering and death. There is no pneumonia but poisoning, that tree trunk could not have fallen on you except by witchcraft; why did it fall at that particular time when you were there, and *you* in particular? No woman is born barren, so the thinking goes; she can be made fertile through treatment with magic or medicine or both. If these fail, a plant or an animal can transform itself into a human child for adoption. (There is a great correlation between accident and quarrel or the state of mind of the person to whom a misfortune befalls or on whom fortune smiles. A happy optimist is in a frame of mind which makes him see most of the things he is looking for; whereas the unhappy, gloomy pessimist is more likely to walk blindly and stumble and

6*

have his worst fears fulfilled. The only way to change such an attitude is psychological: an elaborate ritual. If we want to understand African beliefs we had better approach them through psychology and psychiatry than through religion.)

The moral illustrated by the stories or fables are bits of tribal philosophy. This philosophy, as said before, is taught to every member of the society, mostly in childhood. Some tribes which have age gradations have distinct 'fraternal' and 'sororial' secret teachings. Otherwise the stories are of a standard nature designed for juvenile consumption. Each youngster has not only to hear the stories but must also be able to tell them. When he grows into adulthood he is considered a graduate, as it were. The knowledge and wisdom taught him earlier is no longer a bit of information to be remembered but a tool to be applied. Just as an educated Englishman illustrates a point with a quotation from, say, Shakespeare, a Christian is guided by the Holy Bible, an ancient Greek was a master of his mythology, so an African knew and used his literature. (There were also late night adult stories.)

Some people are more equal than others, even in the telling of stories. For it is an art in itself. There were professional (or official), amateur, and ordinary raconteurs in all tribes. An official raconteur was a minstrel of a sort, travelling from village to village. In every home, however, a mother, a grandmother, or any elder could start off story-telling in the evenings when the day's work and supper were over. This was also the training ground for the children, as they were also expected to tell stories in turns.

Whoever told a story had to apply every means of communication to the best of his ability. He had to be creative. To arouse the audience's interest and maintain it, the story-teller had to dramatize with his hands, lips and teeth and tongue and voice, and the body which was sometimes elaborately made-up. He was a lone one who told a story without asking for the participation of the audience. He might throw a question at the audience or answer one if asked; ask for volunteers to dramatize an episode; or invite a choral response to the songs and the structural jingles. He could also lay the story aside and interject obviously personal commentaries.

A raconteur rarely plunged into the tale proper without some preliminaries. A Muganda would ask a question such as 'Do you know what happens to a thief when he is caught?' as an introduction to the various theft stories about the Rabbit. He might also name his tale prior to telling it so that, if it is a favourite one, the audience would follow it with the usual interest they show when the tale is told. Some tribes have a set form of introduction. The Acholi, for example, require that the story-teller 'calls attention to his tale' (*Ododo na ni yo?*) to which the audience show their readiness by responding 'Yes' (*Iyo*). After which he goes into the story proper which happened once upon a time. At the end of the story he reveals what lesson it was supposed to teach. He then challenges another member of the group to tell another tale. The tone of the story is light, like that of light music. The story is told in a simple diction and in straight-forward sentences. The background, the tales, the characters involved, and the tools used are things familiar to the audience. The method of narration calls for realistic portrayal; even the ten-eyed giant has to be made a mental reality. In whatever language the story is told, the most figurative and colourful adjectives and adverbs are used to paint the picture in bold stripes and loud colours. To make the chief protagonist really exceptional, the story-teller makes use of a sub-dialect consisting of nasality, consonantal variants, and lisping. The mimicking of such a speech is fun, especially in the hands of a gifted raconteur. But all the time the major purpose of telling the story, which is to teach, is not lost sight of. This is taken care of by repetition of descriptions, retelling of episodes, recapitulations, and songs. The songs are particularly effective since they are built up using one verse per episode and go on mounting with each episode till at the end you can practically sing the whole story in the song.

Now to turn to the discussion of the fable and its subgroups. They are explanations of anticipated questions. They are attempts at answering the questions 'what' and 'why': "What would happen if such and such happened?", "Why does this happen?" or "Why is so and so such and such?". The originators of these stories seemed to have gone about answering the riddles of life in the way an experimental scientist goes about doing an experiment to demonstrate a hypothesis to a class. He knew what conclusion would be reached. For the sake of that conclusion, he constructed the whole fable.

A major theme of these tales is: 'A good turn is alway paid in kind,' or its antithesis: 'Tit for tat.' There was always someone to reward a kind deed and punish a wrong-doer. Nemesis was very efficient in putting people in the straight and narrow course.

The moralistic tales are so similar to Aesop's fables that many westerners have wondered whether Africans did not borrow from the Greeks. The truth might be that Aesop borrowed from the Africans by way of Egypt just as the Greek did borrow in other things. On the other hand, nature being uniform in her manifestations to the tropical African and the insular Samian might have led them to draw similar conclusions about life. After all, there are only minor differences between cultures.

Some tales fall into the 'Pourquoi' — for what — group. These are aetiological, and attempt to answer the question 'why'. In this class we classify such stories as 'why the owl flies at night only', or 'why a hunter should refrain from killing animals during his wife's pregnancy'.

Another class is that of demon-lovers, a Cupid-Psyche relationship. In this case a mortal and a demon become lovers. It might also take specific lines where snake women fall in love with men. Closely related to the demon-lovers is the fertility cycle. At those times human life was more valued than now; the greatest calamity that could befall a woman was to be barren. (Those were the days when every woman saw to it that she carried a baby, contrary to our contemporaries who carry pills!) There are very many stories featuring pre-occupations with 'barrenness-cure'. The cures were herbs, ceremonies, and witchdoctor's prescriptions. If none of these could induce fertility to 'come', a plant or an animal would volunteer to become a barren woman's child. Such a child made bargains with his 'mother'. He could, for example, demand that his antecedents be withheld. If this is not observed he deems the contract broken and then reverts to his former nature.

Let us pass over a miscellaneous classification of stories. Some of these deal with children who have magical powers; hunters (the 'outsiders') who go past tribal boundaries and are taught many new things including animal languages, brotherhood of all animals and are sometimes converted into vegetarians; and magical men who are different from others by being only half of a man split through head and chest.

And the trickster tales are the most entertaining, satiric, and humorous. They treat of roguery in the way English sixteenth century picaresque romance stories did. There are differences between the two, though. The tricksters, who are generally animals, are finally caught and punished with a sort of poetic justice. But care is taken to preserve, or revive, the hero for later exploits. A dismembered Rabbit can be 're-assembled' by friendly and skilful small insects. After that the Rabbit runs off to cause mischief elsewhere. Although these trickster characters vary from place to place they gain in effect by the contrast of having a character as small as the tortoise pitted against the elephant. For further distinction, they are given speech impediment. The hero or villain is denied the ability to pronounce sibilant sounds such as in *grass;* or explosive ones such as in *friend* and *don't;* or tricky ones requiring the pronounciation of vibrating *r* represented by such words as *wrong* or *right.*

There are human tricksters and deity tricksters on top of the animal ones. But whatever characters they happen to be, these tricksters are all intelligent, selfish, vindictive, cruel, vicious, and morally unrestrained. They are dangerous to foes as well as gullible friends. As I have mentioned before, the animals chosen as chief protagonists vary from country to country depending on ubiquity and popularity rating. In Nigeria, the chief protagonist is Tortoise, He is married to a small Beetle. Though Tortoise outwits all other animals in the jungle, he is no match for Snail. Ghana's trickster hero is Spider, called Ananse. His wittier son, Kweku Tsin, gets him out of situations beyond his management. East Africans have a young Hare or Rabbit. He has a mother, an unknown or insignificant father and the habit of claiming everybody for a friend or an uncle. Sometimes in these countries, as well as in others, Toad, Mosquito, Chameleon, Cock, Bat, or Owl play major roles. The Hyena is everywhere the laughing stock of every animal just as the many-eyed Giant is the most detestable. (In these years of political campaigns, the political candidate's symbol or emblem is regarded with the respect previously accorded the animal tales.)

If there were no ways of curbing these pranks, the jungle would not be a comfortable place to live in. Fortunately, there are witchdoctors who know methods for catching the culprits. What they recommend to the offended parties may be the building of a tarbaby, or a wax maiden, or a limed figure which is then placed in the spot frequented by the culprit. The trickster's love for the beautiful will induce him to go to make love. Once it touches the dummy or decoy it sticks fast. A hidden hole may be used for trapping it; it might even perish in arson. Nowhere does a trickster escape scotfree.

All that has been written above is an attempt at a brief survey of traditional African literature and literary techniques. That was not done for nothing. It is felt that the various African techniques are being neglected. It is not that we are to revive all things of our past. If a renaissance is just a device for reverting to past modes without justification, it is as good as a retrogression. But there are things you can teach through a fable much better than through a poem or a novel. George Orwell's *Animal Farm* tells us much more about communism than text books which fail to communicate with the general readers. In Africa itself, I bet readers of Jomo Kenyatta's *Facing Mount Kenya* may not remember all the names of the clans, the circumcision rites, and forms of government, but will always remember the allegory concerning man and the beasts of the jungle. The allegory goes like this: Once Man and Elephant were friends. Elephant, through his craftiness took over Man's hut. When Man reported to King Lion, a Commission of Inquiry, composed of Rhinoceros, Alligator, Fox, and Leopard, was appointed. Man had no representation on the commission because his people were considered not educated enough to understand the intricate jungle laws; in any case, he need not doubt the impartiality of the God-chosen gentlemen. The commission found Man wrong and gave the house to Elephant. Man built another house but another member of the commission took it over till he had actually furnished all of them with houses. Man then thought and thought and arrived at the conclusion that 'there is nothing that treads on the earth that cannot be trapped'. He then built a very big and beautiful house. When the honourable members of the commission came to wrangle over its ownership, Man set it on fire and killed all his tormentors. He went home rejoicing saying: "Peace is costly, but it's worth the expense" — a truth borne out by the success of the Mau Mau war.

The fable as a literary and educational means has a great future. It only needs modernization. Tortoise must rent an apartment even on a third floor. We need not take Rabbit to the taxidermist or zoo when we bequeath bow and arrow to the trustees of museums. For Rabbit needs to resume his inter-stellar movements as some stories informed us. In other words we should cast modern conditions in the moulds which are in our traditions, if possible. We the story-tellers being literary men are creative. It is neither our business to tell all the tales, nor calling to relate a tale slavishly; we have to exercise judicious discrimination. The task of collection we leave to the ethnologists. We deal with tales which interest us, which can best explain modern dilemmas and teach us preferences, which instil wisdom, which cause laughter, which unmask modern economic and political tricksters, which create beautiful modern wax maidens for enticing the modern rogues, and which can best establish new codes of behaviour in conformity with our changing situations. By so doing we shall give to literature its central position of education. And, after all, writers are the unacknowledged legislators of the world.

We can dress these tales for classroom and fireside consumption by the use of modern speech and colour. Since ours is a world where past and present, East and West, exist side by side, our tales are bound to bear the brand of this anomaly. We are not children of two worlds; to acculturate us, ingredients had to be borrowed from Moslems, Jews, Christians, Caucasians, Asians, Red Indians, to add to our African base. Our hundred percent African is polycoloured; both the writer and the reader. Hence our stories will be more appropriate to the readers if they reflect the sophistication of the readers. Not only that, the writers are to be more knowledgeable than the readers and should be ahead in intellectual leadership.

In writing our tales or novels, if we aim at a wider readership beyond that of our tribal or language group, we have to adopt English, French, Arabic, or Swahili. Unless we want to create literary curiosities, we shall have to let the small languages die a natural death as others have done before, or leave them for writing regional literature. If it is, say, English we have adopted, we will not have to stick to Queen's English; that is English for people in England. We have to tame the shrew and naturalize her so that she echoes local sentiments and figures of speech as understood by those who attend the political rallies, those who sit patiently before the school-mistress with her cane, and those who search for the mirror that reflects the men we are. A foreigner's English is different from a native's. The difference arises chiefly because of differences in sentence patterns and constructions and idioms. When learning English we are also learning a different thought pattern and philosophy. Sometimes we merely succeed in substituting English words in our native sentence constructions. The manuscripts of unspoilt writers like Amos Tutuola illustrate this, point beyond doubt. Gerald Moore is reported as complaining that Tutuola 'twisted languages into patterns characteristic of nothing except perhaps himself.' But what had Tutuola to do? Why should he forsake his native word usage and submit to the tyranny of English? If William Wordsworth were alive today, he might have urged the gods that reside in Stockholm and bestow literary immortality on men to award Amos Tutuola the Nobel Prize for literature. After all, no writer, including Wordsworth himself, has succeeded in using 'Language really used by men' [and animals!], and dealing with 'humble and rustic life' the way Tutuola has done.

We need not use English equivalents of our figures of speech or proverbs nor do we need to translate elaborately making them lose their epigrammatic nature. Paraphrasing, and transliterating can help. Such a treatment of English will lead to the development of various African English differences in pronunciation, spelling and other ways. These differences will arise from the upgrading of local speech (in the vernacular) into English. The new languages such as English and French have to pay a price for their absorption into the African's thought process. Already the two have been fused with local cement into the West African Pidgin English.

Our traditional literature contains materials and techniques which are not found elsewhere. We need to salvage these and use them in our writing. We are also the people to create new African English and African French. These will give us the facility we need for transmitting our cultures and wisdom. The need for teaching has never been so great. It calls for the employment of all the techniques we know. Thus we need to salvage from the ethnologists' shelves those tools which had been so successful in teaching our ancestors in the past. Traditional African literary techniques can be very successful in creating the successive consensuses and consciences that changing conditions demand.

Negroes are not Africans

The Negro is a unique creature. He is of Africa; and yet not quite. He is of Europe; and yet not quite. He is of America; and yet not quite. But he combines these three disparate strands in his constitution. The confusion which ensues from this combination is the root of all his problems.

In these late days of race pride, he has just awakened to the search for racial, cultural, and historical roots, Hastily, he is likely to pounce on Africa. If he sticks to that, and that only, he is mistaken. For, although African slaves were transported to America three or four hundred years ago, the moment they left the African coast, they were no longer African entirely. Europe, America and the seas determined their fates.

I have travelled far and wide in America. I have been to Atlanta, to New York, to Boston, to Buffalo, to Minneapolis, Minnesota, to Chicago, to Philadelphia, to Washington D.C.; but I have never come across a Negro who looks, talks, behaves, thinks like a full African. Apparently, there are more Africans left among the Negroes. What we have are "coloureds" — in the South African sense of the word — meaning descendants of black African parents and white parents. Hence the Negro is the joint product of Africa and Europe, in America. If he calls Africa "motherland," he must also call Europe "motherland" — or more appropriately, "fatherland." He has the right to be proud of the old African empires of Ghana and Songai. Equally, he must take pride in French civilization, in English empire, in German greatness, in the Spanish Golden Age, in classical Italy and classical Greece. Those are the homes of his other parents. Culturally, he is sub-American, and extremely little African.

There was an act of deception. It went like this: Whites called Negroes blacks. Negroes agreed they were blacks, no matter the amount of black and white pigmentation in their skin. Whites said Negroes came from Africa. Negroes agreed that they came from Africa. The Negro fate thus placed in my hand, I, in my African humanitarianness, have welcomed him. But the Negro is merely my nephew and cousin. Most of the mothers were my sisters, a few of the fathers were my brothers. But the greater number of the fathers were my "brothers-in-law" — the white man in America. Old man it was too bad you sowed your wild oats. You must now take care of my nephews and cousins running about in your compound, as I have taken care of the descendants of African slaves resulting from the internal slave trade.

The act of self-deception continued. Whites have not been claiming rapport with the white-skinned Negroes. Never have Negroes claimed their places in the white world on the basis of the whiteness of skin, sharpness of nose, length of hair, and a common culture. Instead they come asking me whether "I live in trees over there," or have I a tail. It is mostly my cousins who are inquisitive. I don't know what most of the boys think.

The persistence of this myth of Negro origin — that he is the descendant of Africa, alone, has placed the Negro in a four hundred year political, cultural and philosophical jungle. Consequently he has not been able to establish a solid American base for functioning as a full-fledged American. When most parts of Africa were under European tutelage, he (convinced that his home was in Africa only) felt ashamed of his country of origin, of the cannibalism, of the nakedness, of the backwardness found there. Shame for Africa agitated the Black Moslems so much that they left Africa altogether and embraced Arabia as the point of origin of the Negro. And Black Muslim is not yet thirty years old.

In history, it resulted in the creation of Liberia. Liberia as a home for freed slaves, yes; but Liberia as a home for returned Africans, no. Later, Marcus Garvey's Back to Africa Movement, supported not surprisingly by the Ku Klux Klan, was still another act of flight, of despair in hostile circumstances, among half-brothers and half-sisters, all the same.

In those old days of Washington, Du Bois and Garvey, ideological war, the person who emerged with the best record is Booker T. Washington. Washington, realizing that the cards he held in his hands were worth so much if dealt right, showed a political astuteness which his detractors cannot efface completely.

If a politician is one who gets the most for his own people — prevailing conditions taken into consideration — Washington's project of co-ooperation between Negroes and whites paid dividends, and would have paid more if it continued, since it operated under sympathetic conditions. It is a fact of life that — short of a revolution — you cannot emancipate serfs over-night, you can't make all (or most) slaves professors over-night. So, one had to go stage by stage, equip the uneducated with skills that can make them earn now, and strengthen their houses, the houses from which would come the future professionals and intellectuals.

(In the American social strata, the Negro is in the lower caste. Therefore, when thinking about his improvement or uplifting, bear in mind that you have a low caste problem, compounded by a visible colour.)

I do not think the Washington project would have kept the Negroes "hewers of wood" forever. He was an achiever. But Dr. William Du Bois upset the whole thing in his haste for making intellectuals, elites. Part (perhaps he greater part) of the blame for the present poverty and ignorance of the Southern Negro (and those who ran North) should be laid squarely at Dr. Du Bois' door. Du Bois' elites are doing relatively well for themselves. Not so the poor whose lot Washington would have raised.

The confusion of identity still continued. The Black Muslims look forward to the day when the United States will give them a land, part of the Union, rich in mineral, agricultural potential, etc., where they may worship and live as they think best, undisturbed by Uncle Sam.

And the Black Power advocates want to have exclusive areas where they can do things the truly Negro way without the white-man's interference or help.

Americans have pride in their European countries of origin. Apart from the sense of identity this provides, the ethnic (and consequently "social") solidarity pays political dividends through political machines and winning elective posts. The outsiders have been Negroes and Red Indians. Feeling excluded, the Negro has had to set up his own exclusive clubs, counter clubs.

In these post-Hitler years, it may be wondered whether ethnic and racial prides are worthy of perpetuation at all. White Americans, Negroes and South African Whites should wonder.

But, ethnically, the Negro is one better than the African and the European or white American. He has another source of pride either of us does not have. The Negro doesn't have to wait till Africa is dotted with skyscrapers before he acknowledges his African origin. He doesn't have to wait till Europe or white America has claimed him for one of their sons in order for him to realize that the name Mahoney he carries is his passport for an Irish-American club; if he is called Baldwin, he is Anglo-Saxon as well.

Consequently, he should have got into line long ago and marched along with other whites to receive his western legacy as well as to acknowledge his indebtedness to it. He is a European too. The whole European civilization (which began, er, er, from Africa and flourished in Asia before going West) is as solidly behind him as it is behind any white in this country.

Not only that. Negro women should have applied for memberships in The Daughters of the American Revolution. After all, you were here even before The Mayflower, and you have English blood in you. Others should apply as Jews to Bennington College. Others should hold private talks with Senator Edward Kennedy and ask him a typical Irish question: "Ey Man, you ain't gonna leave me out when our next kingdom come, air you?"

But so far, Negroes have been playing at being Negroes, with little profit and much hurt to themselves; with horizons which are poor and mediocre. Their *raison d'etre* has been to be a Negro. A Negro hamstrung by looking at dark Africa and groping for life in the lower levels of America, albeit.

And the bulk of the Negroes have remained penned up in Negro reserves by the New Slave Dealers — the Negro professional politicians. The Negro politicians, the Negro ministers and churches and mosques and gangs are all on equal footings; all are vampires. (Politicians and churches are exploiters everywhere, no doubt. The point is, the Negro counterparts have little to offer to their clients.) And for easier manipulation, the Negro has to be kept low and in one place where he can be reached instantly. And he must know he is a Negro, a descendant of dark Africa who has no share in the present dispensation, except if these middlemen deliver it to him. And the middlemen? They are also exploited. Negro artists and sportsmen are the only people who know where they want to go and how to get there directly.

Actually, Africa and Europe have been struggling for the possession of the Negro soul. And Europe has the greater part. That is as it should be. The Negroes are only Africa's cousins and nephews, in a patriarchal world. Europe, settled in America, dominates the landscape.

The wearing of a moustache is a success for White Power: moustaches mask thick Negroid lips. The use of hair straighteners is a success for White Power: removal of kink. Crew-cut hair is a success for White Power.

A pertinent question could be asked at this juncture: Must one have a racial pride before one can live successfully in this our twentieth century? Must the Negro go to excavate all the old tombs in Africa in order to catch the life spirit to make him function as a human being? As an African, my answer is simple. If you want to be our archaeologists, fine. Meanwhile, I am sending my children to study Keynesian economics, quantum physics, existentialism, Chinese landscape painting, the classics, Danish and Swedish social welfare, as matters of priority.

Rather than go to The Moorland Library, New York City Library, The Library of Congress, in order to look for your African parentage (invariably ending up somewhere in a West African royal family) is it not more worthwhile for you to find out 'who your European foreparents were? There might be a family legacy lying somewhere for you, or one the state took away on grounds of intestacy.

For some twenty years now, African and West Indian intellectuals have been debating the relevancy and irrelevancy of Negritude as a guide for the future ordering of African affairs. Negritude is a philosophy which states, among other things, that the Negro (and African) have certain unique characteristics, and these make him function in a virtuous way, establish relationships with the human aspects of things before the scientific ones; that these peculiarities need be preserved, and need also be placed on the pedestal among the other twentieth century world contributions, guiding lines for ordering of matters; and that the Negro (and African) must function in the peculiar ways the exponents of the philosophy have laid down. Stated in the Negritudist way, it is very confusing because the Negritudists are confused and have shifted ground so much that they are at a loss about the cardinal and immutable canons of Negritude. We shall cut the Gordian knot and say Negritude says: "Negroes and Africans of the world, since you have been rejected and kicked about and your shrines abused, refuse to move any more and declare that you are satisfied with what you have. You have no bombs: that is a virtue; you have no industries: that is a virtue; you had witchdoctors: that is a virtue," etc., *ad absurdum*.

And Negritude is an American philosophy — it was imported into Africa by default, by Du Bois of the United States and Aime Cesaire of the French West Indies. President Leopold Sedar Senghor of Senegal and the former President of Ghana, Dr. Kwame Nkrumah, were the African representatives of this alien and dismal philosophy. It burnt Nkrumah out, and it almost did Senghor in, except that he has recanted.

American Negroes have just received Negritude dressed piping hot by Stokeley Carmichael. So American Negroes (late as Americans always are) are re-enacting scenes from African politics of ten years back. Then Negritude (Francophone Africa) and the African Personality (its version in the English-speaking parts of Africa) were in great demand to arouse the blacks from stupor and political apathy — to arouse them into political activism. In their heydays, Negritude and African Personality worked wonders. After independences were won, we had to roll up our sleeves and get to work — no more luxurious talks. Doing, that is, working to achieve lasting results, is not easy.

Now, when American Negroes woke up to the fact that their plights were not getting any better than those of West Indians and Africans, hysterically they revived Negritude — and named Negritude — and named it Black Power. Black Power, used as an *ad hoc* program, works well in arousing people to political consciousness. But it can only be used as a short-term project — before it turns sour, or worse, poisonous — in the service of a long-term project.

Black Power has no healthy future, just as Negritude hadn't. It will sizzle out sooner or later. The big question is: What, after Black Power? After knocking his head in the *cul de sac* of cultures, Negritude came back and spoke in a new voice and started marching in the direction to the future. "For the future — and this conviction guides a chief of state — " (it is the President of Senegal, and the leader of Negritude in Africa, M. Leopold Sedar Senghor, speaking) "the future belongs to a hybrid civilization." And that is where everybody who knows where he is going — and even who doesn't know where he is going — is going.

False starts — and quite a few of them — have been made in Africa. We may be failing in doing certain things, but most of us know the direction we are going — straight into the 21st century. And to arrive there we are not going to go the way our grandparents would have gone — on foot and by canoe — we shall fly, we shall go by missiles, we shall go with the white man, we shall go with the yellow man. And, we shall go — by all means.

Now, you Negroes who want something peculiarly and authentically African in order to identify with and feel manly, what peculiarly African characteristics will you find in the Africa of the 21st century?

Part of your trouble is that you don't know Africa that well. White America knows more, Negro America knows less. White America is the government and white American officials meet with African government officials. Those Negroes who romanticize Africa that much should take compulsory courses on Africa, read Richard Wright and Frantz Fanon and Rene Dumont for enlightenment.

And when we reach the 21st century we shall arrive there without our kings and aristocrats (isn't that why Nkrumah demoted feudal lords?), we shall arrive there without serfs (isn't that why Uganda kings had to go?); we shall arrive there without tribes (isn't that the test going on in Nigeria, Kenya, Sudan, now?). By the time the 21st century comes — that century of the man of equal privileges — Africa might offer more to each individual citizen while the white Appalachian poor might still roam the hillsides, migrant farmers might still be underpaid, Ghetto Negroes might still room with rats.

The Negro subculture is a culture. But it is essentially sub. Institutionalize it and you have formed a permanent Sub-American culture. Pride in it is essentially an act of despair — and Negritude, or Black Power, if you like — is an act one resorts to when the grapes are slightly above one's reach. But must one be content with a half? Shouldn't one try for more — shouldn't one's reach exceed one's grasp, however elusive that grasp might be? In the mythologies we learn that Proteus will give you his "true" character after all false poses.

I have toured Atlanta (suburb, slums, and all), lived in Knoxville, Tennessee, for a year, lived in South-East Washington, D.C., for three years, roamed Harlem at night and during the day, seen what Phili has to offer, I have walked Boston's Roxbury Negro ghetto — and I have walked with my eyes open, my nose functioning, my ears sharp. Seriously, will any educated (no, that word may not apply very well here) — will any enlightened — Negro come forward and tell me that that is the type of life the Negro must be proud of, the one the white man is not to desecrate? All those week-end drinking bouts?

All those fights? All that vegetating? Mental rotting? All that squalor? God forbid! Are these the repertoires the Negro college students want to nourish and fondle in their exclusive "Soul Tables?"

If I were a Negro, I would go to school in order to place a long distance between me and the ghetto. If I develop complexes in the process, I wouldn't mind. That will be the price to be paid in pursuit of higher ideals. The rise of the coloured world is part and parcel of the rise of the world's workers. Chitterlings are delicious, no doubt. Steak is even better and more nourishing. I would work my way into the American middle class, get myself a house in the suburbs and say: "Ghetto, adieu!"

There will be others who will be active in raising the standards of the poor. There always are. They get their pleasure out of it. Well and good. God bless them if they have convictions and integrity. God bless them if they are Negroes. God bless them if they are Whites. God bless them — the twelve just people.

In most countries revolutions are led by members of the enlightened upper and middle classes who know the best things the establishment could offer but are disenchanted by the amount it gives, the pace it is taking, and the inequality of distribution. These are the people who normally change the systems, or some parts of it.

In India, it had to be the high caste Gandhi to lift up the untouchables. Rome had its Grachii brothers to try to alleviate the problems of the plebeians. In Cuba, it had to be Fidel Castro. Only in America do trade unions fight for their own betterments. Only in America do Negroes have to try to emancipate Negroes. Only in America are Puerto Ricans supposed to solve their own problems. In America people want to dodge the "drafts"

— and let the devil take the hindmost — nobody wants
to remove the "drafts" completely. Those who are
afflicted by these scourges are to try to extricate themselves
as best they can, through self-help projects. Self-help
projects by the poor? the ignorant? the wild? and manned
by the poor and ignorant? If they burn their way out,
who can blame them? We the enlightened ones,
teachers, journalists, politicians, who always knew
better but never lifted a finger in aid?

In India, Gandhi changed the minds of the upper
castes towards the acceptance of the untouchables.
Here, there is no idealist Gandhi, no dedicated Gandhi,
available to soften the hearts of White Power and
change White Intellect.

While there have been few Negro visionaries to
solve American problems, there have been fewer white
visionaries. The only truly dedicated ones are three,
three Southern ladies — Harriet Beecher Stowe, Lilian
Smith, and Carson McCullers. In South Africa Alan
Paton fights with dedication. Here I can't think of an
imposing name of conscience.

It is a fact of life in our 20th century that we are
our brothers' keepers — regardless of whether they
descended from monkeys or were created on the
sixth day, or how they got into their fixes. We want to
uproot disease, ignorance, hunger, poverty, fear, from
the surface of the earth. The hungry have always
cried out for bread, not stones. In order to do this, we
must develop a permanent idealism, an idealism
incorrosable by nationalism, racialism, wealth,
practicality, political manipulation — in a word, an
idealism between hearts.

Harlem is not a Negro problem — not a *particularly*
Negro problem. Harlem is the problem of New York

City, the State of New York, the government of the United States, the citizens of the United States. It is not for the Negro to raise Harlem up. They may help just as any concerned American would help. If the people of the States consider it "beautiful," why, then, let them make it more beautiful. If they feel it is an eyesore, they will uproot it.

Minorities everywhere — in Iowa City, or Lumbumbashi in the Congo — have their peculiar problems. And minorities are of all sorts. Left alone, they cannot solve their own problems. The enlightened members of the majority groups have simply to help.

Uncle Africa wrote a letter to his Nephews and Cousins in America once. That letter fell in the wrong hands — my hands. I will share it with you:

"My dear Cousins and Nephews (it read) :

"Greetings,

"I have learnt lately that you want to instal me as a guiding spirit. Naturally, I am flattered. But I have changed a lot since your fathers and mothers left here some time ago. And now I am changing faster and faster. I don't know which "spirit" of mine can act very well as your guiding spirit. Perhaps keep as much (or little) of me as you can and get more and more into the ways of your new home.

"I am currently engaged in putting up a modern permanent house. The old one was falling apart and we pulled it down in order to have the site for the sturdy one now being built.

"Next time you stop by you will be surprised at the amount of progress we have made away from the dark ages. Those ages were really dark — that's a fact of history; it can't be denied. But we don't celebrate the skull-hunting days any more, just as Hawthorne would not like to see the witch-burning days at Salem glorified.

"From time to time, I shall be coming to discuss matters of state with your chief: Chief Plenty. I have more mouths which need feeding, and I would like to plant enough food for them. I need better hoes, and hope Chief Plenty will spare me a few.

"In your last letter, you complained that you were poorly housed and fed more poorly than your other brothers and sisters. Too bad. To live in the palace of Chief Plenty and yet starve to death! When I come there, I shall suggest tactfully to my host that you could receive better at his hands. Beyond deploring the fact, and wishing my host had done more, I can't do more. Remember, I shall be a guest.

"I understand you want to use Black Power in order to knock certain obstacles down. I thought your Black Power was used up in the cotton fields, civil rights marches, working on the railroads. Don't you think it is high time you used your White Power? After all, you have White Power too.

"You see, Black Power, used as a ram for battering down certain fortifications, works. But there comes a time when the knight has to alight from his horse, sheath his sword, in order to embrace his beloved. And again, some doors open easier with keys, others await a mere push, others are already ajar, and some are always open. Your wisdom will be measured by the means you adopt in each particular case.

"When you are thirsty, lower your bucket where you are. That estuary has fresh water also. I am sure, by now, my in-laws know the looks of a thirsty man, and can give him drinking water without waiting till he has prostrated himself before them.

"Remember, the problem you are fighting is the inhumanity of man to man, of nature to man. If any man comes forward and asks if you need any help, tell him to join in. If any man rolls up his sleeves and comes to lighten your burden without asking you, let him indulge himself. You need every available hand, maximum co-operation, in order to score a resounding victory, a victory over problems, not over man. This is not the type of war to be fought single-handed.

"The darkest night is not that dark. Your grand-mothers and grandfathers saw darknesses compared to which what you see now is morning light. They had hope. Revive that hope and you will cross the remaining rivers towards Jerusalem in a shorter time.

"With love,

"Uncle Africa."

"P.S.

"Cousins and Nephews,

"We do not go skull-hunting any more. In our new dispensation, we have not set up memorials for everything we did in the days past. About some of them, the less said the better. I am saying this so that you don't go re-introducing defunct rites. For, we now play soccer, participate in boxing, and win long distance races. I hope to see you in Mexico City next year when I come to compete in the Olympic Games. If you win more glory this time, I won't let you do that again. In coming Olympics we shall carry all the medals back to Africa.

" 'Bye,

"Africa."

African Students in Washington D.C.

Most Washingtonians have seen at least one African student. There are about 400 in the institutions in the District, most of them are in the colleges, a few in high schools.

That they live among the masses and shake hands with the rulers such as the Secretary of State Dean Rusk, or of an evening walk an American sweetheart to an embassy reception dressed in their national dresses (not "costumes"), is a common story.

Apart from the generalization, what do we really know about them? What are their hopes and fears? What are their views on things around them? What are their attitudes towards Americans, whites and Negroes? What are their problems? How do they find life here?

It is a fact that more Africans associate with whites than with Negroes. It is therefore ironic that more of them get married to Negro girls than to white girls. Furthermore, more of these marriages are marriages of convenience. To my knowledge, it is African men who marry American girls; no African girl has married an American male here.

More West Africans marry Negroes, probably because there are similar characteristics between them which three hundred years of separation and mixture have not been able to erode completely. Nigerians lead in the number of marriages. Sierra Leone, Liberia, Tanzania, Kenya also have sizable numbers of American brides.

Most of these brides, both white and Negro, come from disorganized homes; some of the girls had to act contrary to parental wishes. No African here has as yet married a celebrity as the Ghanaian Joe Appiah did to the daughter of the English statesman, Sir Stafford Cripps. The Daughters of the American Revolution have yet to produce a bride for an African.

Some Africans import their brides from home; others fly their whole family, wife and children, to come to this City. (It is quite a complicated process which draws much upon one's resources, financial and diplomatic, in getting around the tight immigration regulations.)

The unwillingness to marry whites comes from the nature of African politics. (There is still an amount of animosity against whites which wanes and waxes with international problems like the Rhodesian and South African.)

It is easier to rationalize the marriage to a Negro. The common denominators of colour and suffering under whites are primary factors. However, whether the American bride is white or Negro, realities of present day African politics make such families nearly unemployable in posts where the security of the state is at stake.

The reasons why Africans get along better with whites are not far to seek. Some whites are expiating for their mistreatment of Negroes by being good to the

African (another black person, and a non-economic competitor). It settles accounts with their consciences.

Others act from paternalistic and religious purposes: they feel it is their duty to do something for the poor Africans who must be finding things really very difficult in this very advanced country. Some take the Africans for converts to western civilization and embark upon the preparation of the torch bearers.

And just as the whites operate from a well-defined cultural base, so do the Africans. They are therefore bound to find cultural parallels in each other's culture.

Government officials, duty-bound to sell the American way of life to foreigners, just have to associate with Africans. They are more tactful. Some Africans mistake their diplomacy for genuine friendship.

Some Americans are so keen in exposing their liberalism that they want to tote an African everywhere: to church or any gathering like an acquisition for exhibition, especially if he is dressed in his "native robes".

More whites are better educated and more informed about modern conditions in Africa, and have a wider world view than the Negroes. This gives them a better perspective of things and their consequences.

The above remarks should not be read to mean that *all* friendships American whites and Negroes have with Africans are caricatures. Genuine friendships arising out of pure sentiments (unconnected with business, diplomacy and symbiosis) are there, but few.

"Negro" and "African" are words whose connotations have more to do with mentalities than colour. Thus it is not surprising that the African and the West Indian have more in common than with the American Negro,

In Howard University, for example, the little dating that goes on between Africans and Negroes is done mostly in freshmen years. After some time, or when the girls have become sorority members, it dwindles further. The sororities look with disfavour on their members who date non-members of their related social fraternities. The fraternities and sororities which serve American youth as outlets for pent-up steam resulting from social and parental inhibitions, do not attract most African students.

And yet African students meet with more genuine warmth among the less educated Negroes (minus those who straighten or barbeque their hair) than his college mates.

In Howard again, there is a mixed reaction to African students from the professors and the administrators. Some of them show varying degrees of hostility; others are so good they help beyond professional etiquette.

Anyway, the situation at Howard is complicated by the fact that there is generally little coming together between the students, faculty, and administration in the College of Liberal Arts.

The plane on which the African operates is different from that of the Negro.

All talks about the "Brotherhood of Blackness" are passionate expressions of unrefined thoughts. For, the Negro American owes allegiance to the Star Spangled Banner for which he is willing to die in Viet Nam while a Guinean's allegiance is to Guinea; just as a Ghanaian is not a Nigerian; an Indian not a Pakistani; again just as an Indian in India is not the same thing as an Indian who has taken up the citizenship of Kenya. Should a war break out between Kenya and India, he is willy-nilly going to march against the Indian army and shoot. Those are laws of politics, national and international. Political realities rule us, or should.

If we forget that, we are headed for international confusion. Africans can play mischief in America by using Negroes; the United States can use Negroes for mischiefs of her own designs among Africans or the coloured peoples. In fact the case of Malcolm X and African diplomats' misuse of the U.N. by giving Julian Bond a dinner there illustrates one side; the appointment of Howard University's President as the U.S. Deputy Permanent Representative to the U.N. has been interpreted as a means of tapping the supposed good will existing in the coloured world. Senghor's Folly called Negritude and babel called Festival of Negro Arts is also a fertile ground for international intrigue.

It has been drummed into the mind of the African student that he is an ambassador of his country here. Since such a big chieftainship requires a regal bearing, non-committal, and reserved, at times, does this not add to the African's aloofness?

The African student who comes here is select — either through scholarship or through the mastery of finance and other forces. He is therefore likely to be more serious, and an intellectual recluse. He cannot simply fit into the popularity contest that the American campuses are full of.

Some of the Africans are over 40 years old and yet are still struggling for a B.A. with an American kid in his teens.

Africans come to widen their intellectual horizon; but they find the American student generally less serious; the Negro student less so. This, despite the fact that some of these Africans (including this writer) are the first literate generations in their families. As an intellectual, the American is no inspiration to the African in the undergraduate school.

It does not take a long time before African students learn that Americans want to be praised.

This stops them giving free and genuine criticism. Yet the critic and the proponent are equally valuable for success. The critic (especially the foreign one) is better than the complacent supporter or a person who ingratiates himself to the good graces of another.

So whenever they are asked direct questions concerning American foreign policy or the Negro problem, or just the common "How do you like our country?" they are likely to beg the question and address themselves profusely to extraneous matters. As likely as not, they will talk at length about U.S. technological wizardry.

Had they wanted to be honest, forthright, or candid, most of them would have had nasty things to say about certain aspects of life here. (The Nigerian writer, John Pepper Clark, touched some of America's sensitive parts in his bitter book, *America, Their America*.)

Racial problems are less heard of here. Not that they do not exist at all. The landlords and employers are so sophisticated in refusing to give an African a house or job that they cannot be caught on technicalities of law.

What can one say about the barber who refused to cut the hair of an African prince on the ground that his machines are not designed for cutting kinky hair? Or about the African boy who turned down a job because his prospective Negro employer said he had to cut his hair short in order to get the job?

Segregationists they pass over as eccentrics not to be bothered with; not worth the energy of an argument.

They would have wished more American senior citizens had rid themselves of the popular views and attitudes they held on the African in their teens; and the junior citizens had regarded Tarzan as Batman — sensational and ridiculous creations by artists.

One thing the Africans find almost customary is that most Americans who play the Good Samaritan become very able Pharisees in publishing their achievements. This may be a carry over from American political practices where each person is also his own publicity officer; it is not the way to be friends.

For, which African has not discovered that help rendered him in private circumstances has later become a gossip topic or a space filler in a reception? Give casual help, by all means. But leave it casual. If there is an endearment then do not debase humanitarianism to the level of farce.

Whenever you see African students dressed regally, it is not that they are all sons of chiefs or that their fathers own gold mines. They have a sort of stoic philosophy which makes them lock their miseries indoors and strut out into the D.C. streets with shiny teeth: proud victors over their own miseries.

There was that Georgetown University linguistic student from Kenya who was reducing his language to orthography and writing a dictionary. He worked on words and existed on coffee.

There is that Howard University history student who stayed hungry for seven days. No hunger strike, mind you. He simply had no money. The best that a compassionate American family could do for him was to give him their basement to sleep in. He would have possibly died there too had he not been given a check of shs. 5.00.

To keep alive, pay fees and rent, the unlucky many who do not have scholarships have to work. In some cases they meet with more luck than Americans, in other cases they have difficulties getting jobs and doing them.

How is a man who cares more for okra than scallops supposed to cook the latter food? Yet that is what this writer had to do for Howard Johnson's patrons. First of all, he never cooked before because his culture demands only women cook. Secondly, some employers do not take trouble to acquaint the African employee with the nature of the new job and the machines to be used.

The students here do all sorts of jobs: washing dishes, operating lifts, guarding buildings, teaching, broadcasting with the Voice of America, cab driving, to mention only a few. Some of them hold three part-time jobs on top of going to school full-time.

Occasionally you may meet some who have a high sense of business. Take my friend from Sierra Leone, for example. He owns three taxi cabs which he rents out, and are on the D.C. roads twenty four hours a day.

The Nigerians have a way of doing things. It is not a myth that they are richer than other students. They have cars and live in lavish apartments. They have a way of keeping a job too. They introduce fellow Nigerians to their employees and bring in Nigerian successors whenever they are leaving a job. Some employers have had a string of Nigerian employees stretching right back to the beginning of the century.

Our students here have a high sense of what a student's residence should look like. It would not be worth coming to America to live in hovels. In the world's richest country things should be an improvement over those in Britain, France, Russia, or Africa.

After all, what the economist Thorstein Veblen called "conspicuous consumption" may be re-acted by the small man in his small way.

We had a Kenya student here who really needed money to pay his fees at George Washington University. His pride could not allow him to have a cheaper apartment in a poor neighbourhood. Instead, he got himself a nice apartment (fully furnished) in a nice neighbourhood and invited his friends from whom he was soliciting money to come and discuss his financial problem.

They came. True to African hospitality, he entertained them with drinks ("What would you like to have?") and, I guess, food too, to the accompaniment of home music booming from a record player placed next to a T.V.

Well, his friends went away and concluded the boy was too rich to be helped.

Shortly after that, my friend was out of school. He went South where fees are lower. Thus ended the tragic history of a budding black bourgeoisie.

There are Washington D.C. chapters of America-wide African students' national, regional, Pan-African organizations. There are also African-American and international organizations. Each university has at least one of these international organizations.

Some of the national organizations share most of their governments' policies, others do not. Some of them, like the Nigerian and Ghanian student unions have their headquarters in their countries' embassies. The Nigerian Students Union stood opposed to most of the activities of the Balewa regime. Most Ghanaians supported Nkrumah while he was in power and now condemn him, to keep their scholarships (perhaps?), which he had instituted, in the first place, and to keep themselves and their families safe.

Politically, our students here are less active than their brothers, say in Sofia, London, Peking, Dar-es-Salaam, Cairo, Ibadan, or Accra. This is in connection with the amount and intensity of their reaction to the policies and activities of this country or any other country on Africa.

Perhaps Americans may feel glad about this, but its implications are disturbing. Is this apathy temporary and localized to politics only or are the students becoming generally dull? Is this the price for scholarship and hospitality? Whatever it is, apathy is pervasive. In the progressive African countries where a certain amount of extremism is part of politics, these students may lose out to their compatriots trained in their own countries.

Moreover, this is a country where sensitivity against an action is measured by the amount of overt reaction; the lambs may well perish in their silence.

Of course, once in a while, a few demonstrations are held. Some African students spent hours in jail when they demonstrated against the West after the murder of Lumumba.

The regulations regarding demonstrations here may be some of the contributory factors discouraging the students. Last November, angry students had to go to demonstrate against the British government for its failure to block Ian Smith's seizure of power in Rhodesia.

But they had to demonstrate some half a mile away from the British Embassy. It is hoped that by some black (or white) magic, the British ambassador realized that the demonstration was directed against his government and not against any other government whose embassy is situated along the road. Embassies here are so secure.

They do not have to repair broken glass windows!

Generally, the Africans have a broader world outlook than American students, or their brothers and sisters back at home. They indentify more with progressive elements in their own countries and in the whole African continent; they are all supporters of African unity and form the core of non-alignment in its purest theoretical sense.

Some of them do not see eye to eye with their own home governments on specific things. In this respect I have already pointed out the Nigerian case. The East African Students Union has been (and is still) the greatest advocate of East African Federation. Most Ghanaians were as enthusiastic in their praise of Nkrumah when he was in power as they are now enthusiastic in denouncing him.

Those with deeper political and economic insights would wish to see an end to too much dependence on foreign aid. For, if it is good politics, it is also poor psychology; while it spares the muscles it weakens the intellect. They foresee the development of an aid-seeking mentality and the virtual assumption of vassalage by their countries' leaders.

The African student here is often confronted with the question: "What are you going to become when you go home?" or is wished good-bye with the remark: "We hope to meet you when you are the President of your country."

Most of these questions have no relevance to the realities in the African political scene. In the days of parliamentary governments, or in those parts where democracy still rules, yes. But now in the era of army generals, the proper place to ask such questions is

Sandhurst! In other places, it is as if "Papa Doc" is being imitated.

Moreover, only in a few of the countries is it still possible to begin at the top. These are either the newer states, or the poorly developed (by African standards) countries such as those between the Congo and the Union of South Africa, by-passing East Africa.

Positions of leadership, the African students are realizing more and more, are not so open as before: incumbent parliament members are getting entrenched; junior officers are becoming senior officers, etc. So our students will have to accommodate themselves as best they can between the President or Army General and the high school graduate, whether in the civil service or private business. Or work to change the system. In Nigeria, for example, a B.A. is of little importance. In Malawi or Zambia, for example, it still has much value since there are few graduates.

Nothing final or conclusive can be said about the African student here and elsewhere. What we have just done is to expose certain facets of his life.

We may leave this survey with these few remarks: the African student's relations with whites and Negroes are conscious; favours may be done him (or he may be mistreated) because he is black; he is a useful ingredient in the cold war; his home government regards him as a mathematical figure itemized in man-power planning. As yet, he has no intrinsic values.

African Students are Culturally Deprived

Prologue:

(i)

... It is to the French people that I have
known that I trustingly address a piece of
writing in which I have tried with all my
might to enhance the glory of the works of
the human mind.

— Madame de Stael
Preface

(ii)

It is quite possible for literature not to
conform to our rules of good taste and yet
to contain new ideas from which we could
benefit by adapting them to our own style.
It is in this way that we are indebted to the
Greeks for Racine and to Shakespeare for some
of Voltaire's tragedies. The sterility with
which our literature is threatened might
convince us that the French spirit itself
needs to be renewed by a stronger sap.

— Madame de Stael
General Remarks

(iii)

Views that differ from the prevailing
spirit, whatever it may be, always offend
the vulgar mind. Study and inquiry alone can
provide that liberality of judgement without
which it is impossible to acquire new
knowledge or even to preserve what we have.
For we submit to certain received ideas...
because they are powerful.

— Madame de Stael
General Remarks

(iv)

The philosophical system adopted in a
country exerts a great influence upon the
inclination of the mind. It is the universal
mould in which all thoughts are cast; even
those who have not studied it unconsciously
conform to the general predisposition
it inspires.

— Madame de Stael
Philosophy and Ethics

(All quotations from Morroe Berger's
translation of *De l'Allemagne* in
*Madame de Stael on Politics, Literature
and National Character*.)

N.B. I do not expect my readers will agree with many
of the things I have written. But I expect they will be
stimulated or irritated enough to review our
Weltansicht. We have put our best foot forward,
namely, politics; it is not doing very well. What about
those other untried feet?

Africans are the most culturally deprived students in the United States. In the first place, they lack an active classical culture of their own. Then, political nationalistically inspired slogans (i.e. Negritude, African Personality, and other African slogans not yet explored in depth) block their participation in other people's cultures. Opposition to things Americans and Western is another reason that keeps them from exposures to cultural activities in this country. Indifference or apathy or lack of curiosity, and plain laziness make the deprivation total.

To be sure, they dance High Life, Rumba, and the Monkey; listen to Miriam Makeba's singing and Olatunji's drums; watch *Africa Adios* and similar anger-inspiring films; they read Cyprian Ekwensi and Chinua Achebe (if they read fiction at all); and participate in other lowbrow entertainments where they flex their muscles either in laughing or dancing or drinking.

To read a Homer, a Dostoyevsky, a Brecht, a Sartre (unless assigned for class courses) are very rare occurrences. Among their records, a Bach, a Beethoven, or a Tschaikovsky are rarely found. They do not go to watch Mozart's "Don Giovanni," Tschaikovsky's "Swan-Lake," or a play by Edward Albee, or even Shakespeare. They never own a Picasso reprint. They do not, of their own accord, attend lectures on Relativity or Cybernetics.

Admittedly. these things are Western, but so are the civil rights meetings which they avidly attend, so are anti-Vietnam war meetings, so are the hamburgers they eat, so are the big cars some of them drive, so are the popular movies they watch on their TV's, so is the language they use.

113

If these students participated in their own activities of higher culture — things which give breadth, width, and depth to their outlook towards present day life and the world, experiences which sharpen their sense faculties so that they could be aware of more than the superficial — in short, if there were African classics — real and great creations of the intellect — I would not have written this article at all.

As it is, we have intellects grappling with Keynesian economics, quantum physics, plasmas, the various theories of culture growths — people who are in most ways intellectuals, moreover the best brains in their various countries, coming here after having secured competitive scholarships, and people who are potential urbanites, the elite, the bourgeoisie, the ones who will have ample money and leisure to acquire and enjoy the best things that life in the 20th century can offer — these people, I say, still adhere to peasants' and houseboys' forms of entertainment. The crafts that tourists buy, the dances that are exhibited at the Expo 67 are the best they can offer to themselves and to the world.

Compare the average African student to the average Asian student in this country. The Asian has a long tradition of established classics. If he is an Indian, of whatever caste, for the purpose of national pride, he can still take pride in the Indian classics. But whatever African classical dance, classical literature, classical music, classical (divine and pagan) sculpture he had were discouraged or strangled by the colonials and missionaries. (A disssertation on the inquities of the Western and Eastern evils in Africa is of great historical interest, but it cannot help in forging our new cultures.) There grew up two or three generations in a near culture void. One of these generations is composed of these students. The Asian can spurn other people's cultures and withdraw into his own. Where does the proud African turn? In his "boycott" of other people's cultures, who remains the poorer?

The Latin Americans, for their part, derive cultural nourishments from the United States and Europe. In literature and architecture some of them have adequate home products. The African is only proud of his drums and heartbeats.

And the American student who is out to enjoy all that money can buy and culture give, has very many things with which to stimulate himself. Of course, as in all societies, there are these who do not care. But those who care and for whom the universities' cultural committees arrange cultural performances, or for whom theatres and orchestras exist, can have more than their fill. But the African is never tired of the monotony of the bongo drums, the "kwela" whistles, the sweet voice of the Congolese vocalist Rasignal. So he keeps his mind functioning strictly by arithmetical progression. To elevate it to the geometrical level of functioning he never cares to do. Simplicity.

Perhaps there is "a false start" here also? Yes. There must be. And it is the task of African genius (if she has any genius at all) to unearth these "celebrated" false starts and replace them with vistas which lead to other vistas, infinite visions, structures whose roofs are so high our heroes can never hit them however hard they try, dainty stimulants placed so high they (our heroes) have to lengthen their necks giraffe-wise in order to taste them. We also need higher things; things beyond the reach or experience of the vulgar and the average.

Our knowledge of the external world is conditioned by our possibilities of perception. The phenomenal aspect of things, which we tend to take for their reality, is an effect of the limits of our sense perceptions. Senses more refined than ours would show us worlds of atoms, of light, of energy, where now we think we see tables, buildings, individuals. Subtle beings, whose substance escapes our perception, can exist around us, penetrate us, play with us, act on our thoughts and our senses, without our having the least awareness of them. The number of senses and sensations which are theoretically possible cannot be determined. We probably have within us latent senses of which the organs are undeveloped, and which we cannot consciously use, although sometimes a vague and uncontrolled perception may result in some partial knowledge, some otherwise inexplicable "intuition."

For man, the spheres of sensory perception are limited to five (or more) — that is not necessarily true for other species. Therefore, we know five aspects of the external world, which do not necessarily coincide exactly.

Hindu philosophers call these spheres "forms of existence" . . .

Forget the African you are supposed to be. Consider the house of sense organs that you are: an efficiency machine which has remained unused to the point of rusting and which now requires brisk brushing and oiling in order to function as well as others are functioning. Yes, sir, yours is a dormant bud. Or a field that has remained fallow through generations and generations of villeins, plebeians, peasants. Yours are organs that need to be developed to function as organs capable of coping with life in the 20th century. In order to sense, your sense organs have first to be developed. Yours are eyes that became useless in your confinement in darkness. Now you are opening them, just opening them like those of a young pig or rat, and you are only able to see silhouettes and blurred outlines. But there are more things in this world than are dreamed of in your narrow philosophies, in your Medieval cosmologies and witchcraft.

The human machine can adapt itself to any condition; it can take any pose; it can act any role. Either it makes various adjustments and lives or it goes the extinction way. Either it keeps the resilient philosophy of the Negro, or it keeps to the rigid philosophy of the Red Indian and dies with all dignity. But once you are dead, you are dead, and there is nothing more to be done about it. Maybe, you become a tragic hero for drama.

For the sheer exercise of the mind, for the glorification of the human intellect, for the extension of the field of human awareness, or what man can achieve, can't you lend your mind to various conditionings so that eventually your mind or the minds of your associates and children will help show man the varieties upon varieties of things in this world? In fact, your minds, collectively, are fresh and vigorous, not having been bombarded to insensitivity and cloying as those of older or retired nations such as the Portuguese and Spanish, Greeks and Romans.

You, sir, swaying to your *Kwela* music in your Harvard dormitory, are you better off culturally than your brother in Kilembe mines? Does the brain within your head explode with the vigour of a Beethoven symphony? Or does it prostrate like an Indian music, or the whining of a Negro spiritual? A rich find just mined, which your brain is, should contain enough power to make a Geiger counter needle oscillate like mad. Brains, you know, can be conditioned to function according to the "normal fundamental laws of over-acute consciousness." Many can be (and are actually) abandoned to vegetate. These compose the "scum" of humanity.

I believe in the evolutionist theory of cultural and social growth. With an elaboration here and a trimming there, it is the best explanation there is of how man's ways came into being. Man's culture had a single beginning just as the species man evolved from a single beginning. Since no convincing theory has come forth to show that the various groups or races of man evolved from so many subhuman groups, the theory of evolution of mankind from a single source is a better explanation, for me. If man, or the intellect in man, developed from a single origin, man's cultural evolution follows automatically: it is therefore the continuation of evolution in his ability to perceive, explain, and impose an order.

Reader, if you are too sensitive to the words "savage," "barbarian" and "civilization," you had better bypass the following quotations. I am going to tap the matured Tylor and Morgan vintages. (There is more to be learned from these pioneers, who are often discredited as arm-chair scientists, than many would expect. They saw far, and clearer than the younger breed who followed them and who have confused the anthropological atmosphere. Above all, they were not so avid in the use of euphemisms, like "developing" for "underdeveloped" — the bane of the moderns for humouring us — we who quarrel about names but not facts.)

Now, Edward B. Tylor said in 1871 in *Primitive Cultures:*

> By placing the European nations at one end of the social series and savage tribes at the other, and arranging the rest of mankind between these limits ... ethnographers are able to set up at least a rough scale

of civilization ... representing a transition from the savage state to our own.

Man is no longer sacred. God is dead — his death came through the mortal wounds inflicted by Darwin. Nietzsche only announced the death to a disbelieving world, a group which had underestimated its power of successfully fighting its father's authority. There is no longer a "sacred" origin for man, and not even a Victorian age (after Freud) with its rules of good breeding which constrained T. H. Huxley going the "whole Urang." If man came via the Urang Utang, via the amoeba, need will lose face when it is also said that man was savage and barbarian?

Lewis Morgan wrote in *Ancient Society* (1877) :

As it is undesirable that portions of the human family have existed (were found existing — my correction) in a state of savagery, other portions in a state of barbarism, and still other portions in a state of civilization, it seems equally so that these three distinct conditions are connected with each other in a ... necessary sequence of progress ... the domesticated institutions of the barbarous, and even of the savage, ancestors of mankind are still exemplified in portions of the human family with such completeness that, with the exception of the strictly primitive period, the several stages of this progress are tolerably well preserved.

However, I have to state my position. It is this: After the first man (men and women) evolved, it stayed in one area and evolved the rudiments of culture (and maybe a common language), but for some reasons, the settlement was broken up and various groups fanned out, travelled, passed through various new places carrying with them the cultural rudiments. As they travelled, passed through various new places which had their own fauna and flora, climatic conditions, physical features (phenomena) they modified their ways of and outlooks to life (or had these modified) accordingly. Hence the variety in the human species. Because some of these groups faced hard hurdles to surmount, their brains answered the challenges by becoming more acute, agile and persevering, and active. So their minds evolved as their cultures evolved. Others had good times elsewhere and had no need to fashion wings for flight from danger or towards distant unknown goals. These remained savage. Separate developments (or lack of them) continued all the time the various groups were lost from one another. When brothers met brothers eons of years later, some brothers were doing well, and others were not. Since the reunion, these brothers have been asking themselves and one another whether they were once brothers, how they got separated from one another, when the break took place, and wondering why their fortunes had differed so. And that is all the education man is getting in the social sciences and the humanities.

And the differences between the evolutionists and the anti-evolutionists is this: that the evolutionists start from fundamentals whereas the others move from branch to branch like monkeys who cannot grapple with the tree stems, or dig down to the roots of things. The evolutionists are Platonists, and the other group Aristotelians; they are Freudian while the others are Jungian: the one group expands its energy digging into the roots of things, the other elaborates on secondary characteristics, or comments on verses in the text without a desire to reduce the whole text to its fundamentals.

Ease of communication and trade induced brother to search out brother. Although one brother had become prosperous, all brothers had punched in equal time, year in, year out. One brother used his time more meaningfully. All brothers can learn one another's tricks. And that is why African students are in the United States. My complaint is that we are learning (if at all) very, very few of the tricks of our brothers. Our brotherly reaction at meeting this prosperous brother is a withdrawal into ourselves. Our stalwarts, who tell us to withdraw by using a twist of logic, are with our richer brothers. They are putting on weight nightly, and acquiring substance, too. But we others are being restrained by the myths they ordained. Can it be that our brothers know the virtues of brotherly pats on the backs, but selfishly want them for themselves? Yes.

And that's the tragedy. African politics is as modern as the other human activities. Politicians make use of modern technology in counting votes and disseminating propaganda. African politicians get advice freely, from Syracuse and elsewhere. Now show me an African Pragmatic philosopher after Whitehead? African students who studied in France and Germany are in a philosophical jungle (all philosophies are jungles, but the one we are talking about is a jungle of jungles). Where is our existentialist philosopher? Instead we have such resolutions passed in the Paris Conference of Negro Writers and Artists (1956):

> We recommend that artists, writers, scholars, theologians, thinkers and technicians participate in this historic (perhaps 'archaeological' and 'antiquarian'? — my own query) task of unearthing, rehabilitating and developing those cultures so as to facilitate their being integrated into the general body of world culture.

I am sure they omitted mention of 'politicians' advisedly. Erratically, they proceeded:

> We affirm that all peoples should be placed in a position where they can learn their own national cultural values (history, language, literature, etc.) and enjoy the benefits of education within the framework of their own culture. (The madness of Black Power apartness; a subtle revival of Booker Washington's separate but joined — my comment.)

My dear sirs, good sirs, gullible sirs, isn't the present 'framework' for everybody from Japan to Alaska, via west, one 'framework,' namely 20th century? In any case, one very successful politician has an answer to all this 'jungle' talk. He said clearly that he was not ruling his country according to the ways of our grandfathers, but according to ways learned in school, the ways the white man brought. We are living in a world conditioned to a large extent by the white men. Either you fall in line or go scaling all the stages in cultural evolution.

After an interval of four years, these jungle dwellers, prodded under the ribs no doubt, had to call upon

> ... the African philosopher, faced by the totalitarian or egocentric philosophers of the West, to divest himself of a possible inferiority complex, which might prevent him from starting from his African *being* to judge the foreign contribution.

Need we worry more about these 'philosophers'? (How many are they?). Professor Willie Abraham teaches philosophy, and teachers of philosophy are not necessarily philosophers; and apart from providing a commentary on the thoughts of Nkrumah, his book announces no new philosophy. President Leopold Sedar Senghor started off justifying Charles Dickens' Negritude on the false anthropological — missionary and theological anthropology — as hybrid an anthropology as Marxist anthropology is — premises. After continuing ticking until he crowned his false premise with the fanfare of a festival, he cried off, in a recent *Africa Report* article (February 1957). He writes:

> ... When I was younger, I would gladly have come forward as the spokesman for all Africa, or at least for Negritude. *But now experience has taught me the diversity of Negroes and Africans, and it would be presumptuous of me to speak in the name of either.* (Italics mine).

For obvious reasons, I am excluding all political biographies and papers, most of which are ghosted. What we need to worry about is not the "possible inferiority complex" of the African explorer of implications, but the bigotry and rapacity of a pig, which makes her eat her young. It is the difficulty of removing the beam from our eyes to enable us to see the mote in the others. We should fear more the dictatorship of the ignorant and the ancients in our midst and the prophets who spoke languages which are dead ends.

Frantz Fanon, are you with me?

African, let your mind soar. There are millions of paths your likes have never travelled before. Challenge all masters. And beat them. Why not? You are *not* underlings.

The ideas of the sacred, the taboo, the ritual, the soul, the divine, with their oughts and privileges, rights and wrongs, are the arbitrary creations of man's ancestors in ages past — creations of past poets in poetic flights of imagination — in attempts to regularize lives, activities, times. Each society needs to redefine the area of the sacred. And each man has to define the area of his own sacred. Learn to love yourself more. Be your best counsellor. You are *that* sacred.

African 'philosophies' now are just mere slogans for the market place: in other words, we have tourist or 'pop' philosophies.

Most Africans have been and still are, as plebeian as Luther was, with well-marked distaste for what they didn't have or what are above them. We need a Calvin to come with a mature sense of business — we need someone to come and tell us that: Indulge yourselves in any and everything FOR THE GLORY OF AFRICA.

BREAK THROUGH THE GREAT BARRIER OF INDIFFERENCE AND UNAWARENESS, OF MEDIOCRITY. BECOME SUPERSONIC. BECOME IMPRACTICAL.

> *Il ne suffit pas a un sage d'etudier la nature et la verite; il doit oser la dire en faveur du petit nombre de ceux qui veulent et peuvent penser; car pour les autres, qui sont volontairement esclaves des prejuges, il ne leur est pas plus possible d'atteindre la verite qu'aux grenovilles de voler.*

> — Julien Offray de la Mettrie
> *L'Homme Machine* (1748)

Let's overhear Stevie and Davin.
Stephen: "... When the soul of a man is born in this country there are nets flying at it to hold it back from flight. You talk to me of nationality, language, religion. I shall try to fly by those nets."

Davin: "Too deep for me, Stevie .... But a man's country comes first. Ireland first, Stevie. You can be a poet or a mystic after."

Stephen: "Do you know what Ireland is? ... Ireland is the old sow that eats her farrow."

Africa has many historical things in common with Joyce's Ireland. Irishmen of talent moved out to consummate their creativity. The question for Africa is: shall we create and perpetrate conditions which kill our talented few? Is this pervasive nationalism or Negritude — this philosophy for the layman — this dictatorship of the average — to become the sow?

We laugh at the whiteman who goes to "see" flowers and insects in Africa, or who studies our music. But in this country we have no curiosity to make us interested in what the "natives" are doing. John Pepper Clark in those moments when he boosts his ego, refuses to draw a distinction between levels and degrees, puts the frog and the elephant on a par, and calls the conductor, Leonard Bernstein, and the New York Philharmonic: "Bernstein and his boys." Country and town rats.

Yet very little of the country is remaining unaffected by the town. And when our students are back, they want to be served part of their city "menus." And that will consist invariably of the entree. No desserts.

Can't AID aid? After all, you have collected the "cream" of Africa here and will have them under your charge for four or more years. Instead of remaining practical, falls, winters and summers, I am sure an accent on culture during the summers will widen the vision of the students. And Homestay Families could go shop for clothes in the mornings and shop cultures in the afternoons.

If some of these students could work with theatre groups, music companies, with art museums, rather than with Head Start (without started heads!) in Harlem or South East Washington D.C., they could help in the future in founding the African theatres (national and community) of tomorrow. Because, on top of the cultural experiences, they also learn organizational techniques. One might not want to see a play by Eugene O'Neill, but one can surely learn a lot about conducting a play by working with a theatre group producing O'Neill.

As for theatre, novel, musical and some other cultural facets in their modern trappings, they are the inventions of non-Africans. The African who would like to make his mark in these will have to study the American musical, the English novel, the European theatre or the Japanese Noh theatre and their developments. No way out. If he wants to make variations in accordance with conditions prevailing in his country, he yet must learn the fundamentals.

A major reason for the low level of African literature now is not that the writers do not know literature, but that their cronies, the Africans whom they want to impress — their immediate audience, that is, leaving out for the moment the anonymous audience out there — their friends, those whose opinions they value, and for whose benefits they "act at being writers" — have low literary standards. An African novelist writing in this country might have to traverse half the width or length of this vast country before he can find an African who knows literature or cares that much about it, to consult.

As for the poet who still rehashes Negritude themes, he will have a ready audience. He who can raise laughter will also have an audience. That's all.

And when these thousands return home, they will still be that much uninterested. And they cannot act as the enlightened audience — the catalysts — for the serious writer.

And when an African dramatist adopts a Greek audience (in lieu of an absent African audience) what cries do the hyenas and jackals put out? "This is not African!" But then most things are Greek to most of them.

In Nairobi, the capital of Kenya, a few Africans who are very concerned about the absence of theatres, found one now with enthusiasm and see it dying in their hands the next day for lack of support: no actors, no audience. In Kampala, the capital of Uganda, we have the well-known magazine *Transition* published. But its pages contain articles (politics mostly) and a few poems, and sometimes a story *in two issues*. In the East African countries which I know better, there is hardly an African theatre-going group with the result that the few plays produced by he University students and one or two other groups attract more whites than Africans; and only in those casted by whites do we find an increase in African attendances. And those are facts.

Evidences? (a) Lennard Okola, *Nexus 2*, Nairobi: The present relative boom in the East African literary field needs every possible encouragement, not only from publishers but also from readers, for authors can hardly thrive unless they have a large home audience eager to buy and read. *On the whole, the reading public in East Africa is still extremely small,*

and it is not just the problem of illiteracy. Many of
of our educated people find it more rewarding to
spend all their spare time and money on things other
than books. (Emphasis ours.)

Lennie, it is not only books they don't buy. They don't
watch plays, see art shows, attend discussions, etc.

And the cultural contribution of these educated people?
Evidence? (b)

> ... in the meanwhile (the publisher) remains praying
> that more educated people who are adequately
> employed — teachers, business executives, civil
> servants, academics, etc., will feel the urge to write
> not for money but for the aesthetic pleasure of
> creation ....

Lennie, we hope they will do so, and sooner.

Evidence? (c) Elimu Njau has had exhibitions in
Paa ya Paa, the indigenous cultural hub of Nairobi, from
all sorts of people. All sorts?

But Paa ya Paa has yet to show the work of University
students. Even back at home there the students are as
culturally lost as here. Let's go on —

> It is also indicative of *something* that there is
> not a very large number of student members of Paa
> ya Paa from the University (Nairobi College) ....
> The University students can help to make Nairobi
> more real than it has been.

Those are the observations of a concerned adult back
in Africa about the cultural poverty among the African
students there. Elimu Njau concludes his *Nexus* 2 article
with this last evidence:

> (d) The future of Paa ya Paa and other similar
> institutions and ideas will depend not only on the

persons who are in them today but also on those who will come later to give fresh support to those ideas, and we may anticipate that the task of broadening and securing the base of movements and institutions such as Paa ya Paa will be a slow and often a discouraging one. Just how much awareness there is among University students will be one factor determining the strength of that future support. Probably a decisive one.

Absolutely.

And we have Ministries of Culture; Ministers of Culture; Deputy Ministers of Culture; Permanent Secretaries to the Ministries of Culture and long lines of bureaucrats. I thought that these Ministries of Culture, as well as doctoring the popular cultures, would raise their gazes to higher horizons.

Russia's greatest literary age was that nineteenth century era when she was defining her relationships with western culture. It is in such critical ages of revaluation of all values, both old and new, that we get some lasting statements made and visionaries found. One of these statements came from the pen of the greatest religious and cultural nationalist of that era: Fyodor Dostoyevsky.

His *Underground Notes* contain this truth:

> The only gain of civilization for mankind is the greater capacity for variety of sensations — and absolutely nothing more.

Dostoyevsky knew western civilization, culture or philosophy inside out. His pronouncement is a topping on of western civilization. And because he knew another culture well, he knew Russian culture better. The acquisition of another vision helped him: he could see his own culture in its correct perspective. In order for us to appreciate what we have to the correct degree, we have to have standards other than our own to measure them by.

Now, what is there in western classics for an African? You may ask. I answer: Everything. As Keats said — "a thing of beauty is a joy forever." A true thing of beauty is a joy forever — and for the whole world. Under the surface behind the words, there is a silent language understood by everybody. To communicate in that language you do not need even to speak with new tongues. It is that language which makes the Hottentots respond to Bach's music; Picasso to Congo masks; Romans to Greek culture; Africans to Jewish Christianity or Arabic Islam; why Ghana schoolboys know by heart Shakespeare's "Friends, Romans, countrymen...."

In the final analysis, after you have stripped the African of his acquired Africanness, you are left with an individual who ticks the way all the other human organisms the world over tick. And just as some pigs are better than others, one of these would tick the way Shakespeare ticked, if the conditions were favourable; tick the way Einstein ticked, if he could be allowed to develop his potentials to the highest; tick the way Lenin ticked if conditions were not adverse.

And in this world of ours which is becoming more and more specialized, "guild languages" are going to be the major languages spoken by men. Just as world politicians have their summits and the U.N., writers have their PEN, trade unionists have their federations, hippies their lingo. And these are "tongues" which know no national or language barriers. Are we going to let those sons and daughters of ours who are capable and interested in learning these primary languages have the chances to learn them? Or shall we gobble them up if they cannot remain "Africans"?

The highest aim of all cultures is universal manifestation.

Ezekiel Mphahlele paid pilgrimage once. This is his report:

I visited Britain at the end of June 1959. At the end of my four and-a-half months' vacation I literally ran out, in a state of near-neurotic tremor. . . .

I was determined to lap up as much cultural entertainment as I could. Apart from a symphony orchestra in Johannesburg which gave a few scattered near-charitable concerts for non-whites in poor non-European halls, I had never heard a live symphony concert; nor had I ever seen a big theatre, except for a single *Hamlet* performance given to only blacks in a small theatre and student performances at the liberal University of the Witwatersrand. (Johannesburg).

So I went to ten plays: Charles Langston's *King Lear* at Stratford, one at the Royal Court, one at Regent's Park, and the rest in the West End. Then there were five Proms and a Vienna Boys' Concert at Albert Hall, four musical occasions at Royal Festival Hall, including a piano recital and the concert version of *Don Giovanni* (by far the most moving musical experience I have ever had), and an open-air symphony concert outside Kenwood House. I took thirty-two films in good *stride,* many of which I should never have smelled in South Africa or in Nigeria: the former because of the colour bar, the latter because of an utter lack of sophistication and an enlightened cinema-going audience. *(African Image.)*

No other African can say that. Few non-Africans can say it.

Great works, cultural or technological, are testimonies of the heights to which the mind of man can reach. Africans, stretch your minds — for the glory of the human mind.

If your Africanness cannot absorb many new things, in short, if you have stopped to evolve, then you are like that proverbial tortoise who could not take more in the year of rich harvest because her shell had already determined her capacity. You might also develop an Armadillo complex which caves you in, makes you withdraw within your shell *where you will find no comfort.* We live in a world of varieties upon varieties of depths, widths, and lengths. Either we experience these, or we legalize ignorance and poverty and hunger.

Keino the runner made himself by hard practice. Mohammed Clay the Champ practices hard. So did Charles Dickens, Shakespeare. So did all great artists, writers, actors, musicians, philosophers. Of course, they had an over-sensitive constitution — so do we, proportion-wise. And they also had a high degree of schizophrenia, of sadism, of masochism, of egotism, of exhibitionism. So have we, proportion-wise.

What we need is a philosophy appropriate to our time. A vigorous philosophy to dislodge the medieval and peasant Negritude. And this new philosophy I name Synthesism. To reach synthesism Africa had to feel the impacts of the East and the West, with their influences in various degrees. These affected her traditional ways of life. Africa also has to live in the twentieth century: a century with the easiest means of communication: communication media are in plenty and they reach everywhere, underground and above ground, knowing no boundary whatsoever and defying time. Therefore one can no longer shut off the outer world. Our dilemma has to be seized by the horns; no more withdrawal into a pristine age and praising our ignorance and powerlessness the way the Negritudists did. We are to face the twentieth century, and ask our children to choose their roles and to act them maximally. The present and the future is theirs. The word is Synthesism.

Japan, the Land of the Rising Sun, was the land of the proud. The defeat she faced in the Second World War was the greatest blow to her pride she had ever experienced. But she quickly came to terms with the new realities, and adopted a Japanese synthesism. And she now stands among the first four great industrial countries of the world. And industry is the measure of success — even politics will one day be "industrialized" through cybernetics.

The point is that we need to adopt positive policies for confronting new situations, if we want to make our marks. Hence Synthesism.

Postscript

It pays to read old visionaries. They spoke of ideals which need to be pursued every day. For example, Marcus Garvey started from the correct assumption that an African could become anything, and be the greatest in his field. And I have been exploring the IMPLICATIONS — conjugating the verbs, persons, tenses, and places — of the text concluding this article. In a sense the whole of this article is an exegesis on this text. Marcus Garvey:

I asked, Where is the blackman's government? Where is his president, his country, and his ambassadors, his army, his navy and his men of big affairs? I could not find them and then I declared, I will help make them. My young and ambitious mind led me into great flights of imagination. I saw before me then, even as I do now, a new world of black men, not peons, serfs, dogs, and slaves, but a nation of sturdy men making their impress upon civilizations and causing a new light to dawn upon the human race.

We sought the political kingdom and found it. Now let us add everything unto ourselves.

Lawino is unedu

(A running commentary on the major aspects of
Song of Lawino: a Lament, by Okot p'Bitek,)

* Okot made a mistake in translating this work from
Acholi into English. He insists on spelling Acholi Acoli.
Perhaps if he feels strongly about Acholi orthography, he
should take steps towards its standardization. In view of the
fact that he is very sarcastic about the very, very (the
double emphasis I am sure he would have used) poor
translation into Acholi of religious books by Catholics
perhaps he should have done better. But he seems to have
done worse. Sometimes he imitated the Catholic catechists by
merely exchanging Acholi words for English, disregarding
the sense and the idiom.

* As early as 1954, our author was already working on
a book called *Te Okono pe Luputu.* or something of the
sort. It was in Acholi, like his novel *Lak Tar.* Then, he was
also active in Uganda National Congress.

* *Te Okono pe Luputu* (positively translatable as:
Respect the Ways of Your People, or, Stick to Acholi

10*   135

Customs, or, Blackman, be Proud of African
Traditions — and Don't Abandon Them for the
Whiteman's) was to be in the tradition of Negritude
literature. And, in fact, it is Negritude literature, if the
Song of Lawino is the translation of that work.

* Then he left Uganda and went to play football for
Uganda in Britain, remained behind to study Education
in Bristol and later Law at Aberystwyth. I don't know why
he studied law since he was never called to the bar.
Perhaps it was to acquire legal acumen, perhaps to
improve his mind, perhaps it was a false step. A false step
in the direction of politics. In any case, when the national
elections of 1962 were around, Okot came back to Uganda
to try his chance in the morass of Acholi politics. He lost,
like the other U.P.C. candidates in his constituency.
The constituency was won by a D.P. candidate.

* And off to Oxford he went to read Social
Anthropology. In other words, the Negritude in him
wanted to be given a chance now that the politician had
had a rough time. And, of course, he still had *Te Okono pe
Luputu* unfinished. And what was better than immersing
oneself in Social Anthropology if one was going to attempt
to justify the ways of the Blacks in the eyes of the world?

* Let us add that when Okot came to Uganda in 1962,
Geraldo (Gerald Moore, of course) had organised
the Conference of African Writers, in Makerere. Plenty of
people were invited from many parts of Africa. Okot was
not one of them. I suspect he attributed Geraldo's

136

oversight to the fact that Okot's own works, a translation of a biography of Dr. Aggrey, and the *Lak Tar,* were in a small local language. Is it possible that he might have resolved then and there that the passport to international writer's conferences is a major language such as French or English?

* In any case, Okot went and finished his studies in anthropology and came back to Uganda. Taught in the Extramural Department of Makerere College. Wrote poems, one of them, published by *Transition,* is very autobiographical. Wrote articles on Acholi Love and folktales. Criticised anthropological books on African aspects of life. Some of these sociological and anthropological writings are insightful, others do not show much width or depth of scholarship or perception. A strong charge, I admit. But for Okot's future interest, or for the direction of others who might want to become fully intellectually engaged, such things need to be said, and said now. I might be too severe. But I see more of the frivolous and more of the jester in these works. Only rarely do I see an Okot with tight lips and protracted visage.

* And he founded the Gulu Arts Festival. And in time he became the Director of Uganda Cultural Centre. Meanwhile, he had been revising (we hope) *Te Okono pe Luputu.* He had also been adding to it another or other chapters. And meanwhile, had also been translating the work into English. It had to be translated because that way it would reach more people and could definitely rule out another chance of a conference oversight. So, the *Song of Lawino* came out.

*   That was the Cultural Champion side of Okot, scoring successes. And the political side got more and more restless. It had already jutted its rough head in *Song of Lawino,* section 11. To me, this part looks like a new addition. It is an addition which has less to do with culture than with politics, the politics of success and complaint. In it he inflicts heavy revenges over politicians. The reasons are there: politicians were fighting each other more than fighting the forces of hunger, disease, ignorance. But these very politicians frustrated Okot's chances of getting into Parliament (in all countries, politicians fight each other or the other groups more than the social evils they are supposed to remove).
And, I have already pointed out, the successful candidate in Okot's constituency is a D.P. member. It is likely that the D.P. is disparaged more than the U.P.C. in this chapter because Okot was having his revenge.

*   Of course, Okot is also very serious. Serious as a politician. Serious as a man who wants to see the right things done. In other words, he is concerned. The political Okot is many times stronger than the Social Anthropologist Okot. If the politician in him speaks, the social anthropologist keeps quiet. One day the socialist spoke. The next day the sociologist was reduced to naught. The socialist Okot wrote a revolutionary article in *Transition* which I am told caused the driving of Okot

the sociologist out of the Directorship of the Uganda Cultural Centre.

*   The politicians have had their revenge again. Perhaps Okot should transfer more energy to feed Okot the sociologist. Okot strikes me as being a loner. Unless he can find followers who are willing to try new 'Un-Acholi' things, and unless he can find people as dedicated as he is on certain matters. (Never mind all the crocodile tears which Okot made Lawino shed profusely, for Okot is a sceptic on the surface and between the lines). If he has any other overriding passion beyond living life, it is politics. Religion went with the throwing away of his former Christian name Jekeri. And total commitment to Acholi culture went with the decision to translate Lawino's tribal lay into English: the language she despised her husband for using. It is only with intellectual interestedness and disinterestedness that he can get involved heartily in culture now, apart from living it to the full.

*   It is our present fate that most of our intellectual energy is being burnt up in the dismal trade of politics.

*   By translating his own work, he kept as much of himself in it as nobody else could have. But, as he also admitted, he ended up by clipping the wings of the eagle. He did this so much that the eagle can now fly less than its normal pitch.

*   He gives us the names of those from whose help he benefitted. Well and good. But I wish he had consulted some hoary-headed Acholi Nestors, for it seems to me that he concentrated his search on almost one generation only,

139

and that, his own. Since he advocates the use of oral sources in African social science, does that methodology not call for specialists and a varied distribution of sources of information?

*   Okot has not yet grown out of the old-time *ngala pa luMican ki LuMicon.* Whenever he directs his barbs against the new religion, it is the Catholic catechist he is locked in unfair fight with. And even here, it is with the Catholic translation of catechism into Acholi that Okot makes fun. To him, this translation is poor (from English or Latin to Acholi, that is.) But Okot's own translation of that catechism into his Acholi-English (for that is what Okot is using) is no nearer to the original English or Latin or Greek or Acholi. Perhaps there is a great need for an Acholi *la Micon* to explode this *la Mican* afflatus. Perhaps East Africa's great literary events will come when we get Drydens, Popes, Byrons, Juvenals, writing satires. By then, we shall have converted our deep animosities into intellectual and literary fights — to be fought with the pen rather than with bullets and detention camps.

*   From the moment Okot embarked upon the translation of *Te Okono pe Luputu* into *Song of Lawino,* he had already forsaken the message for the medium. It was literary honours he now sought. The upholding of Acholi virtues has already been forsaken. Lawino will never hear her *Kijira* except in a gramophone record, or over Radio Uganda, broadcast by the victorious Kelementina in our newfound tongue.

*   I don't know what Ali Mazrui finds in *Song of Lawino* to call it an important event. *Song of Lawino,* all considered, is an event but not the East African event. A popular event, yes. A great event? Yes. Since there is literary drought. Translation: the meaning is lost — the meaning of deep Acholi proverbs are made very, very light by their rendition into English *word for word,* rather than *sense for sense,* or *proverb for proverb.* So Ogot has devalued Acholi *gagi* for a trifle English ten cents, at a time when even the English pound is devalued. (Mazrui, check your tastes and values.)

* Too much space and energy (the little there is in this light literature) is taken up with pointing out the foibles in the Western ways of life — these foibles that are easily seen by the eyes of the simple, *unedu,* uneducated Lawino.

* Africans have been mad at expatriates for taking the African 'houseboy' as the representative African. Okot hasn't done better by letting a mere catechist criticise the West and the Westernization (he rarely touched upon the Easternization through Indians and Arabs and Swahili — which are also to be reckoned with) of Acholi, in Uganda, in East Africa.

* The trouble with his method is that his discussion is conducted in a low key: it is the simple that he deals with (the girl is limited both in vocabulary and knowledge of complex things,) and he leaves the discussion of basic Christianity, basic Acholi religion (and basic many other complex things) aside — we are treated to 'tribes' of 'dungs' on latrine walls (Ministry of Works, please check), 'red' lips — things to be seen with the eyes, things to be heard with the ears, or felt with the skin — but little to be felt with the intellect. (Lawino had lost out on intellectual

development long ago.) So, Okot also suffers from the Negritudist impediment of rhythm above sense.

*   I had expected an epic; I got a ballad.

*   Andre Malraux has written *The Temptation of the West*. (Even this is limited in scope and depth.) Perhaps it is high time somebody wrote *The Temptation of Africa*.

*   Ocol (— Son of Ocol or Col: Son of Black, Blackman, African). Names and points like this ought to have been foot-noted, otherwise the non-Lwo speakers will not get the full significance of things since there is no other way for them to do so. Through lack of judgment, some insignificant things are foot-noted.

*   'Who has ever uprooted the Pumpkin?' should have been footnoted. To anybody who does not know this idiom 'Pumpkin' could be a variety of weed.

*   'Words cut more painfully than Sticks.' — That is perfect.

*   Ocol's tongue is 'bitter,' 'hot,' 'fierce,' 'deadly,' 'ferocious,' 'corrosive'. Rather than condemn Ocol for his tongue, should we not praise him for his manhood, his possession of these spears in his mouth with which to fight the new versions of Ocol's wars? The sharp spear must be there, and it should be sharpened by computer machines. Against what object the spear point is to be directed is the decision each warrior will have to make and face. Those bulls with strong arms will fell the elephant. There are others who can hunt only *anyiri*.

142

*   He (Ocol) says "Black people are primitive and their ways are utterly harmful, their dances are mortal sins, they are ignorant, poor, and diseased!" Yes, Ocol, Black people are primitive, their ways are harmful, they are ignorant, poor and diseased. If they were not ignorant, they would not go to school; if they were not poor and diseased, they would not be asking for foreign aid; if their ways were not harmful (to progress) they would have been less primitive. For why did others advance, if their ways were not conducive towards the progress we are now chasing?

*   I have the feeling that Lawino is the doomed villain of her lament, and that the whole thing is an ironic praise of Ocol by his anachronistic wife. Poor girl! Anyway, women come and women go. So be it.

*   P. 21 Ocol rejects the old type.
          He is in love with modern women,
          He is in love with a beautiful girl
          Who speaks English.

I admire your choice, Ocol. All Uganda is behind you in loving English. You don't have to be the one to uproot the Pumpkin: time and natural causes can take care of that without your incurring the curse. In any case, what curses cannot be cleansed?

*   P. 22 Clementine, the new breed, uses make-up which Lawino frowns upon. I wish Okot had given Clementine time to strike back. And Ocol. Why not a trilogy? Lawino had *Pala, moo, ceno, lajaja, akuku, tiko kedo, etc.* As for powder and lipstick, I would advise the cosmetic makers to research into matching colours for the

black-woman's skin. We are all artists — women more so, having their bodies as canvasses. These Clementines with lovers, jobs and leisure, and money, need distractions and diversions and ways for spending money. By God, let them paint themselves pink. By God, let the government tax them dearly for it. By God, let the tax money be used for educating our children.

*   P. 24 Perhaps she has aborted many,
               Perhaps she has thrown her twins
               In the pit latrine!

Good for her. I wish she had thrown more or had rubber collectors for the sperm. (Make your contributions towards population control.) (You young girls going to school, use contraceptives. They are particularly good for students. If by bad luck you still get pregnant, abort every month, as every socialist should. Africans call themselves socialists, don't they? And continue working your way toward degrees, money, and a husband for your later days.)

*   P. 26 (She) walks as if her shadow
               Has been captured.

Poor rendition. "*Woto calo tipu ne,*" or "*Woto calo kimako tipu ne.*" ',Ghost," or "spirit," expresses the lack of life much more forcefully.

*   Pages 7 through 30 contain the quintessence of things Acholi. It is the most philosophic and poetic part. It is the "healthiest" Negritude I have come across.

144

I am not unfair to my husband,
I do not complain
Because he wants another woman
Whether she is young or aged!
Who has ever prevented men
From wanting women?

Who has discovered the medicine for thirst?
The medicines for hunger
And anger and enmity
Who has discovered them?
In the dry season the sun shines
And rain falls in the wet season.
Women hunt for men
And men want women!

When I have another woman
With whom I share my husband,
I am glad.
A woman who is jealous
Of another, with whom she shares a man,
Is jealous because she is slow,
Lazy and shy
Because she is cold, weak, clumsy!

The competition for a man's love
Is fought at the cooking place
When he returns from the field
Or from the hunt,

You win him with a hot bath
And sour porridge.
The wife who brings her meal first
Whose food is good to eat,

Whose dish is hot
Whose face is bright
And whose heart is clean
And whose eyes are not dark
Like the shadows:
The wife who jokes freely
Who eats in the open
Not in the bed room
One who is not dull
Like stale beer,
Such is the woman who becomes
The head-dress keeper.

I do not block my husband's path
From his new wife.
If he likes, let him build for her
An iron roofed house on the hill!
I do not complain,
My grass thatched house is enough for me.

I am not angry
With the woman with whom
I share my husband,
I do not fear to compete with her.

All I ask
Is that my husband should stop the insults,
My husband should refrain
From heaping abuses on my head.
He should stop being half-crazy,
And saying terrible things about my mother.
Listen Ocol, my old friend,
The ways of your ancestors
Are good,

Their customs are solid
And not hollow
They are not thin, not easily breakable
They cannot be blown away
By the winds
Because their roots reach deep into the soil.

I do not understand
The ways of foreigners
But I do not despise their customs.
Why should you despise yours?

Listen, my husband,
You are the son of a chief.
The pumpkin in the old homestead
Must not be uprooted!

Here, the seriousness is authentic. If the song were like this throughout, it would have been great.

* P. 30 How shall we treat the figures of speech? Literal or word for word rendition gives us only the framework. Yet one must entrap the sense, the meanings, the freshness of the original. What is needed is a live animal in a zoo and not a museum piece. How to catch the animal and convey it to the zoo alive are the marks of intelligence.

* P. 32 When the drums are throbbing
And the black youths
Have raised much dust
You dance with vigour and health
You dance with spirit,
You complete, you insult, you provoke

147

You challenge all!
And the eyes of the young men become red!
Red with sex! The dances were sexual, sublimative, therapeutic, arousing the desire as well as consuming it. But the vigour of it leaves the body whole. Too whole, too healthy, I fear. For modern life, modern progress, you need doses of neurosis! In any case, these will come.

*   P. 37 There is no respect for relatives;
           Girls hold their fathers,
           Boys hold their sisters close,
           They dance even with their mothers,
           Modern girls are fierce.

But, as you point out, unwittingly, this 'fierceness' is not new to Acholi. Labeja, the Jok of Alero, (he catches even his relatives) is symbolic incestuousness among Ocol's own people. It had been there before the White men came with their ways. Okot, there are sexual deviates in Acholi who are native breeds. I submit this. The *Lujogi mamyelo dyewori* are nothing other than sexual deviates, and neurotes.

*   Lawino's criticism of Ocol shows her naivete. We do not, of course, expect she could fathom her educated husband. Cultural activities change with socio-politico-economic conditions.

*   P. 47 Like beggars
           You take up white men's adornments,
           Like slaves or war captives
           You take up white men's ways.
           Didn't the Acoli have adornments?
           Didn't Black People have their ways?

That's a point of contention. Did the Acholi borrow ways from among themselves, or not? Did the Acholi borrow from other Black People, or not? Have the Acholi, or Black People, made cultural contributions to other people, or not? If the Acholi and Black People have been 'borrowers' and 'lenders,' what is the rationale for imposing limits to borrowings and lendings now? Unconscious cultural absorptions take place every day without the reasoner's knowledge or sanction.

*   P. 48 And there is not a single *bwola* song
That you can dance,
You do not play the drum
Or do the mock-fight;
At the funeral dance
Or at the war dance
You cannot wield the shield.

Ocol does not care for these. Why should he? He can't practice the "mock-fight" because he is not going to fight that kind of a fight; he does not care about the "war dance" because the war he is fighting is not fought with the same rationales, weapons, or for the same goals. The *bwola* is now a museum piece: a dance danced for its own sake, for display purposes to tourists, or for earning money. So is *myel otole*. *Otole* is no longer a practice for bush confrontations.

*   Chapter Six is frivolous, verbose. Perhaps the word play (in Acholi) and the recounting of the experiences of an 'Unedu' with the complexities of modern life, for a village Acholi audience, was foremost in the author's mind. For 'us' — (Ocol's classmates) a lot of editing and cutting out would have been in order. (In fact, there is plenty of childishness in the whole thing. Some of it is fun for an Acholi audience, some impudence, some sarcasm, and plenty of 'raw' social anthropology. Juvenility, basic, simple.) Simplicity and sarcasm are its strength. Perhaps he wrote *Te Okono pe Luputu* in 1953 or 1954 as *lok oree,* and *arony*. The anthropological part is light reading. Ruben Anywar's work *Acholi ki Ker Megi* on the Acholi is mature, in contrast.

*   P. 99 The moon "elopes" — literal Acholi for '*por*'. The meaning intended though is 'the new moon has appeared."

*   P. 99 Woman "seeing the moon" means to menstruate. — But you have to know Acholi to translate these.

*   P. 100 I do not know
> The names of the moons
> Because the Acholi
> Do not name their moons.

Aren't there seasonal activities and weather conditions which take place fairly regularly in each month, every month, every year, and which were used as names for the months? A week doesn't necessarily need to have seven days, nor a month 30, nor a year 12 months. Were there no Acholi astronomers who observed the sky and could associate the presence of certain stars in certain parts of the sky with particular seasons? There were. But Okot has already tripped himself into the idea that the Acholi had no conception of division of time. The concept of Time in Acholi has yet to be explored.

*   P. 105 A person's age
> Is shown by what he or she does

It depends on what he or she is,
And on what kind of a person
He or she is.

No, there was a norm against which one's character
was measured. And activities. These were the "Age Groups,"
and responsibilities connected with them. Although the
Age Group gradation was not so rigid as in the "Bantu"
tribes, it was there.

* P. 106 My husband says
Before this man (Jesus) was born
White men counted years backwards,
Starting with the biggest number
Then it became
One thousand
Then one hundred
Then ten, And when it became one
Then Jesus was born.

This is wrong. It was that Jesus' birth was deemed
important enough to be considered the beginning of a
new epoch by Christian fathers, long after Jesus was
born and had died. So they made the new era begin with
the year of the Birth of Jesus and counted everything
after that date as so many years after Jesus' birth. Every
event which took place before Jesus was born was counted
as so many years before Jesus was born, or so many years
to the year of Jesus' birth. As a matter of fact, these people
computed wrong by four years! The question is: in matters
of fact, apart from error in mathematical calculation,
should a writer introduce confusion? It fits in well, though,
with the spirit of the poem.

* It is one thing to praise your own cultural values;
it is one thing to counter-pose your cultural values against

another's; it is also something else to recognise that the other culture is already a synthesis (and made development on it) of your own and others; it is something else to buy or adopt the end product of your own sweat, of other's sweat, which has been developed beyond the individual stages of borrowing; it is also another thing altogether to be able to live well in the present with all its complications. If you think ahead, you will be able to absorb all there is, have intellectuals come into your country, keep potential "brains drain" home.

* We feel lost after we have gone outside the known boundary of knowns and accepteds. Re-entry is sometimes suggested as a cure-all. But it can't be done, there is no way for total forgetting of the new. So, we have to let interaction take place. In the hope that things will settle down, adjust themselves, the spirit will be invigorated, revitalized, resuscitated, subjugated, — but will live and gather strength and energy and go on living.

* On the intellectual level, I admire their (African politicians') apparent astuteness; on the humanitarian level, I condemn their deception or hypocrisy; on political ground, they did rather well for themselves; on foresight they were rather shortsighted because their system has a rigidity. Nowhere else in the world have politicians deluded themselves that they are so great as in Africa. The renascent masochists.

* To ask if we had culture is to ask an elementary question. After it has been answered with a 'yes' — does that conclude the discussion? Should it? What needs answering is: What sort of culture had we? If culture

152

is the general manifestation of the group spirit, did this spirit have a great future? Did this spirit have within it potentials which could be exploited by its members to the best of their abilities and to the utmost of those disciplines (branches, paths)? Did this general spirit allow for the utmost individual search for himself and his expression of his individual spirit — unhampered by social, cultural, moral, governmental restrictions? Did it have within it mechanisms for survival — for blending with others, for intermarriage? And the rise of Ocol's people into becoming world exploiters?

*   If there is famine today in India, and many are dying, more are being made barren, we have to blame Indian Classical (Negritude) philosophy for it. Virtue rested on thought, state of mind, attainment of total communion with the gods and bliss; with little thought left for labour. In the days when the caste system was standing strong, the Brahmans could doze away for hours in Nirvana, sure that the slaving class was hypnotised enough not to rise up in rebellion and cut their necks like chicken. Modernization came. And a strange man also came: Gandhi. Gandhi broke the caste system, making the lower caste people as proud and purposeless as the higher caste lazy people. He disrupted the Indian economic system: released the workers without giving them a new purpose in production. Then he did the most anomalous thing in his life: he loved the wheel — the spinning wheel — above the tractor. (The wheel still reproaches modern Indian choice of new instruments for new lives, on their national flag.) So, to wheel — cottage industry — in the age of mechanization. The cow was still sacred, the Gandhiji ate only vegetables — cottager's garden products — and meat. Things more economy-fetching were relegated

153

into the background for reasons of spiritual and cultural health. Each Indian was to go and dig his own salt; —how can we have commerce without exchange?

* So, Gandhi retarded the mechanization and industrialization of India for years. Even now, with Nehru's countermeasures, the Gandhiji's spirit still rules.

* If Gandhi had not been so Negritudist, and had advocated a marriage to the new, couldn't India have been very near Japan in industrialization? If Gandhi had borne in mind that enclosure of agricultural industrialization poured many people to the city and others to industries, couldn't India now be more productive?

* But no. True to his native values, true in defence of what are 'eternally good' and Indian, the Gandhiji could not forsake the wheel — the wheel that has no beginning and no end, the wheel that is static.

* Chapter 8, a sceptic's criticism of Christianity, translations of the Catechism. Lenient on Protestants. Severe on Catholics. Facetious on the ways of Ocol. And in Chapter 9, also black humour.

* P. 174 Chapter 10 is supposed to be a discussion of death, above all. It could have been the end of the book:

> White diviner priests,
> Acoli herbalists,
> All medicine men and medicine women
> Are good, are brilliant
> When the day has not yet dawned
> For the great journey
> The last safari
> To Pagak.

* Chapter 11. This is newly added. It is an interpolation, written since Uganda became independent. Okot with a political temper is better than Okot the sceptic posing as a champion for dying and dead customs he doesn't believe in. These are useful only as means for giving free play to sarcasm, and making fun of other people's ways in mock-revenge for their destruction of the ways of his own people, again in which he does not seriously believe.

* Chapter 11 is the only part written with enthusiasm. It is the only part of the book which has worth because it has relevance to the political games The Sons of Black have locked shoulders in.

* The question I have been asking myself is: Why didn't Okot expend as much intellectual or psychic energy in the anthropological essays as he has done here? Corrolary to that: Aren't Africans now burning up too much intellectual power in the dismal game of politics? That maelstrom has swallowed up many would-be geniuses. But they will also have their honour who excel in the world of mathematics; they will also have their honour who make scientific discoveries; they will also have statues built who transplant hearts; they will also have their days who compose serious music; poets will also be honoured beyond Uganda's border. Let politicians play. Do serious work. Whatever it is.

All said, Lawino's song is commensurate with her comprehension and vision. But, till Kelementina tells us how she lured Ocol away from Lawino and Ocol tells us what he found wanting in Lawino so that he preferred Kelementina, the tryptich picture of modern Africa will remain incomplete.

Here are songs which should be sung by many people of various view-points.

Tutuola, son of Zinjanthropus

Teachers of English language and educated Africans who pride themselves on their mastery of English will be surprised to learn that in creative writing grammar does not count very much. In art, too, perspective, proportion, symmetry, have very little importance to great artists. And, in modern electronic music, the innovations are such that Ludwig von Beethoven would have raged to madness were he to come to life today. Perhaps the arts are undergoing a greater revolution than they went through in the romantic period. Now, some of these modern artists who are transforming our sensibilities, burdening language with a tug and a twist, mangling limbs, experimenting with colour, and time, and tone, and surface, and space — some of these people are ordinary mortals like you and me; they steal away to their artistic world and then come back to us. But some of them live in one world only — their artistic world, full of Alices, Guernicas, Joseph K's, Finnegan's Wakes, and Complete Gentlemen. Their world is not balanced, not as orderly as we would have designed it.

Now, in all that he has done, Amos Tutuola is not *sui generis*. Is he ungrammatical? Yes. But James Joyce is more ungrammatical than Tutuola. Ezekiel Mphahlele has often said and written that African writers are doing violence to English. Violence? Has Joyce not done more violence to the English language? Mark Twain's *Huckleberry Finn* is written in seven dialects, he tells us. It is acknowledged a classic. We accept it, forget that it has no 'grammar,' and go ahead to learn his 'grammar' and what he has to tell us. Let Tutuola write 'no grammar' and the hyenas and jackals whine and growl. Let Gabriel Okara write a 'no grammar' *Okolo*. They are mum. Why?

The arts branched out of the esoteric mysteries of the kingly-aristocratic-priestly class in the beginning of society. When the artist seraed the noblemen, he had to use the language understood by them, he had to use words and expressions which did not offend them, he had to have an aristocratic theme, so he wrote on chivalry, and wrote epics. For a change, he wrote pastorals to acquaint the nobleman with the lives of his shepherds. Everything that could be done to satisfy "Our Most Gracious and Mighty Princes and Lords" was done.

Then, romanticism bursts upon the scene, democracy comes along, and what do we hear? William Wordsworth says the most revolutionary thing there is in the arts: the poet is "to choose incidents and situations from common life, and to relate or describe them, throughout, as far as possible in a selection of language really used by men, and at the same time to throw over them a certain colouring of imagination, whereby ordinary things should be presented to the mind in an unusual aspect." — The encounter of kings in the Crusades is out, courtly love is out; the life of the beggar is in, polite language is out; the labourer's ungrammatical English is in, the Professor's English is out; Pidgin English is in, exact reporting is out; distorted imagination is in, classic poses are out; cubism is in, religious veracity is out; tall, grisly, thronged stories are in.

And yet Wordsworth did not really know the language spoken by men, nor did he know the lives of the common man of England. It is through Emile Zola in France that we view the lives of the new creatures spawned by the industrial age. It is Zola we must take with us as a guide around Kisenyi and the slums of Nairobi and Dar-es-Salaam. If we want to know the common American's speech, it is Twain's Jim, Huckleberry Finn, Tom Sawyer to whom we must listen.

Yet these were educated writers who took leave of our educated world to record the secret lives of the poor across the street. Although they exhibited vulgar forms of life, communications in vulgar tongues, we realize our writers were putting on a show— for our benefit. We know they can speak 'grammar' as well as we do, we know they know many things besides, we are comfortable in the knowledge that they are of our own class — writers who have struggled hard to master the language, master the art of writing, as well as master *their* language for art: language of the lower-classes. Their art did not come to them by chance, it was acquired through the various hard stages we ourselves have gone through. So we respect them and we reward them.

To our surprise, one day, into the hall of the fame walks a primary school boy, a naughty boy, a boy who knows no grammar, almost a total villager, and he claims a seat among the immortals. What? we shout. Who are you? When were you in Achimota? Perhaps you were at Ibadan with me? Have you been-to? In a land where school knowledge is extremely important, our drop-out is meticulously analyzed, weighed, and found insolvent. Our analysts pull their *agbada* up and set to jollof-rice and gari and chicken legs in their university halls and blame the whole thing on Dylan Thomas, Gerald Moore, and the whole White world. "If this fellow (they mumble, not even mentioning that name, to them accursed) had been to Oxford, and had then decided to use his mother-tongue's syntax, like Okara, perhaps we could believe him But ..."

Unfortunately for them, art is a very strange beast, stranger than some of Amos Tutuola's. Art is no respecter of education. Alexander Pope was already mumbling in numbers when he was a tot; Mozart played the piano when he could barely reach the keys; Walt Whitman — that expansive American visionary — who was he, wasn't he just another bum, but a bum who bumped on a face reader and was told that from the look of his facial features great things could be expected of him?

Art also changes its shape more than Proteus. With the classicists art was more exact than a photograph, her secrets were not for us to divine. Michelangelo Bournarroti and his predecessors glorified the perfect man in the name of a perfect, powerful God. But that cosmology has been shattered, the mirror of life has been broken. The world is in bits and pieces; the reflections from the broken mirror have so multiplied things, that we are dazed. In the arts, we have seen (among others) Emily Bronte, Vincent van Gogh, Miro, Nietzsche, Chagal, Pound, Ionesco, Antonioni, Barth, Marshall McLuhan, L.S.D., and *bhang*. Not even Freud himself can assemble the various pieces on his magic couch.

To expect classical conformity is not the thing; to expect classical clarity is not the thing. You can't even expect to find order in language itself. What you can do is to stare at a glass at a time, catch a glimpse of the moving leg, another time stare at the heavens (if not yet clouded by smog), pass from one electrical terminus to the next, and, if you are strong enough, shut yourself in your desert mind and meditate a while. Leave the search for order and meaning to the fools.

Today when the machine is taking up more and more of man's former dominion, isn't it refreshing to find a man who is man enough to stand up against the machines? For what is language but a machine, and learning grammar makes us more and more slavish to it? As a Lewis Carroll character asked, Who is to be the master? Let men say their says. If there are things of importance in them, we the vegetables will be forced to learn their languages in order to get at their meanings. Each writer has his own language. Just as abnormal psychology has taught us more about life than normal psychology, so, a complete system of abnormal language can shed more light onto some obscure parts of life.

Everything that goes on in the world has an effect on us, on how we see the world. We Africans have changed in many ways since the great encounter with the European pioneers. We have felt the impact of Europe, America, Asia. Asia, America, and Europe have not felt the impact of Africa very much. But they are beginning to feel it. I am not talking about politics. I am talking about ways of life and objects of common usage. Now, African fashions are copied by French designers. African languages are being taught abroad. African English, and, yes—even Tutuola's — is being taught in England. And those who learn these increase their stock of knowledge.

Unfortunately, Africans (of the Negritude breed) have always thought they are a different variety of mankind — they were the ones to produce perfection, and any African who did not answer to it had to be disowned.

There are, we should remind our fellow brothers virtuous Africans, vicious Africans, perverted Africans, meticulous Africans, lazy Africans, uneducated African geniuses like Amos Tutuola and Field Marshal Okello, the Father of Modern Zanzibar.

But when has a prophet met with honour in his country? (Runners are a breed apart, since Kipchoge gets his dues.) Jealousy stops aspiring prophets from yielding the palm to an especially dangerous competitor. What these foxes do is to clip our eagle's wings so that he may fly a middle course.

Writing about Robert Burns, another uneducated genius, Thomas Carlyle, said:

> It is difficult for men to believe that the man, the mere man whom they see — nay, perhaps painfully feel — toiling at their side through the poor jostlings of existence, can be made of finer clay than themselves.

And didn't Ben Jonson (another university wit) make it a special point of telling us that Shakespeare "hadst small *Latine,* and lesse *Greeke*" — in the tradition of intellectuals (?) eclipsed by natural geniuses?

Rare pearls have been thrown among us and we have trampled upon them.

Christina Aidoo, after blasting this spoiler of West African reputation in English, this confuser of school pupils with his bad grammar, at least admits, grudgingly, that he possesses an abundance of imagination. But, it is IMAGINATION we seek in an artist.

Education drives out of the mind superstition, daydreaming, building of castles in the air, cultivation of yarns, and replaces them with a rational, practical mind, almost devoid of imagination. Some of these minds, having failed to write imaginative stories, turn to that aristocratic type of criticism which magnifies trivialities beyond their real size, they fail to touch other virtues in a work because they do not have the imagination to perceive these mysteries.

Art is arbitrary. Anybody can begin his own style. Having begun it arbitrarily, if he persists to produce in that particular mode, he can enlarge and elevate it to something permanent, to something other artists will come to learn and copy, to something the critics will catch up with and appreciate.

In 1952, then, we see our young David, clad only in a loin cloth, and armed only with a sling, step into the arena to do battle with the philistine, the Giant, slayer of the Sons of Fame. I was young then — only another boy in Standard 7 — otherwise I might have gone to drag David out of so unbalanced a match. As it was, my heart missed one beat — a beat I have never recovered. But, confidently, he swung his sling and lodged the' stone in the Cyclops' eye. The great beast fell. I thought he was dead, but no, Cyclops had nine lives. May this missile, computer-directed, sixteen years afterwards knock him down once and for all!

Wale Olumide, a Nigerian who throws big names about without establishing a connection, accuses Tutuola of stealing his plots from Jung. This is an ironic flattery. But it must not stick, because:

(a) I don't think Tutuola knows Jung, or knows him that much; in any case (b) Tutuola has no use for Jung, for his materials and tools are home-grown — the very ones that grow around the African shrine or fire-place; and (c) it is from native story tellers like Tutuola that Jung got the evidence for his conclusions.

Chief D.O. Fagunwa, a fellow Yoruba, preceded Tutuola in writing and publishing stories. The chief had the misfortune of being old-fashioned and writing in

163

Yoruba. Now, he is suffering in the hands of inept translators. Undoubtedly there are very many African oral story tellers. Undoubtedly they could tell the stories better than Tutuola, just as other Greeks could have written (might have actually written, but their efforts got lost) better *Odysseys* than Homer. But we have no time for all these 'could have,' 'might have' hypotheses. We demand immediate evidence, right now, into our own hands, so that even the Thomases among us can touch the scars.

If Tutuola trades in African myths and folk-lore, can we credit him with originality and imagination? Yes. For the artist's material is the very earth you tread on, the very traffic accident you see, the very mourning your unlucky neighbour is going through, the very turbulation that agonizes lovers, the very fear of darkness and noise you had as a child. The artist appropriates all this common stuff, and in the depth of his imaginative funnel, transmits it, so that the finished material which emerges at the end of the conveyor belt is a gem whose lustre shines at the appropriate spots. There is nothing new under the sun; says Iconoclastes the Preacher.

Hesiod did not plot the *Theogony*, although he put a Hesiodic outlook into it. Virgil's *Aeneid* is as Roman as Homer's *Odyssey* is Greek, though both told the same story. Had Ovid not been a rake, his *Metamorphoses* might have had less sensuality or passion and — sex, in them. Brecht's plays are transformations of other people's works. And the Great Shakespeare, how many plots did he steal?

When Ariosto presented his patron, the Duke of Ferrara, with his epic *Orlando Furioso*, the duke's only recorded compliment is the question: Where did you gather all these fantastic stories from? Maybe the duke did not know. Amos Tutuola knows the exact order in which he arrived at the various towns in his novels.

Adolf Hitler did him the favour of starting World War Two. He went and worked as a blacksmith in the airforce division. Now, an aeroplane is noisy — and readers have to take their ears with them into Tutuola's jungles; there the very skulls make hideous alarms, audible from miles away. One of his heroes is so handsome a work of art that the very Gods and Goddesses of Beauty bewitch guns so that they won't fire to kill him however hard the triggers are pulled. If Burns borrowed Milton's *Paradise Lost* in order to study the character Satan, Tutuola borrows books on electricity in order to — to what?

Tutuola, Gerald Moore has told us, writes in the monomyth tradition. Some of his episodes, in the clarity of their telling, the sheer imagination behind the work, and their total emotional effect, are as good as F. Scott Fitzgerald's best, especially the *Diamond As Big As The Ritz.* Get a story by Jorge Luis Borges — *The Immortal* will do — read it through and through, compare it with a Tutuolan arrival at one of his towns, you will find that Borges is a mere draughtsman, a cynic who dazzles us with marble throws, but starves our emotions. Get out Franz Kafka's stories or novels, and you will get sick, witnessing self-flagellations of a sick man. But a Tutuolan hero goes through hell with assurance, magic, and a smile. At the end of his 'inconsequential' ordeals, the hero emerges wiser, if not richer, as well. Of him only can it be truly said: Hell where was Thy Sting? Isn't this the very optimism which fortified the African slaves across the seas? Which made them endure what killed the Red Indians in their own land? Which has made the Negroes multiply and prosper in the New World?

Fagunwa's hero Olowo aiye is the "Rich Man of the World", who periodically goes adventure-hunting in order to acquire more wealth. His motto is: Aim for the Best, the Most. Tutuola's hero wants to discover all the secrets of the Gods, aiming eventually at becoming wiser than the Gods. And he actually beats the Gods in their own game. Now, tell me, reader, which Greek God would have tolerated such human arrogance? Zeus of the Aegis? With his Thunderbolts he would have made a mince-meat of such a mortal as a lesson to other mortals, and to surfeit his thirst for blood. And Jehovah the Revenger would not only have smitten such a man, he would have punished the man's descendants to the *nth* generation.

Philosophies vary in their attitudes to things according to prevailing states of abundance and scarcity. Where things — foods, mostly — are hard to come by, austerity measures are adopted and stronger penalties imposed on malefactors — all in the name of Zeus or Jehovah. In the lush tropics where fruits feed the hungry, one is assured of abundance, or near-abundance, and one can afford to defy society and the gods — one knows famine can't last for long, and, therefore, nature is playing a wasted game. Yoruba gods were weak because the Yoruba were stronger men. In their mythologies, man triumphs over the gods. Perhaps they defy the gods because they know the gods are fictions.

Love is the cancer that eats at the entrails of all of Ovid's characters — from Zeus right to the servant girls. Tutuola's characters love in a healthy way, they have a place for love, though it is lower than that occupied by their other endeavours in life.

In our disdain — mistakenly, all the same — of Amos Tutuola, we run the danger of disdaining the very material he worked with, to wit, African mythology. If we do that, we shall have cut our very umbilical cord, and disowned our mother. The social world as we know it originated in myths. Myths are the means for apprehending the world, comprehending it.

We went near and far in order to find parts with which to fit up Tutuola. We realize he has been seen 'incomplete.' And if we can now assemble the various limbs, fingers, eyes, ears, etc., together and assemble our hero, how does the Complete Tutuola look? Not as distorted as Moore thinks! What we behold is a modern ancient: the optimistic, daring, and defiant African of yesterday who could have walked with Beethoven to write this piece of impudence:

> Kings and princes can turn out as many professors and privy councillors as they please, grant titles and ribbons, but they cannot produce great men, minds that rise above the human herd and whose task it is to make themselves, for which they must be regarded with respect. When two men like Goethe and myself walk together, these great lords must be shown what we hold to be great. Yesterday, as we were walking back, we met all the Imperial family, we saw them coming from afar, and Goethe let go my arm to get out of their way onto the side of the road. No good arguing with him, it was impossible to make him take another step ahead. For myself, I pulled my hat down over my eyes and bore down on to the very centre of the company, hands crossed behind my back! Princes and courtiers parted and stood aside, the Archduke Rudolph took off his hat to me, the Empress was the first to salute me; their lordships *know* me.

Lewis Nkosi, note this: Tutuola has the right to miss an appointment with you, or me. He is a genius and the Father of Modern African literature: West Africans woke up to write nervously because he was already in the field, and he is still ahead, far, far ahead; East Africans have lately entered the field. South African writing never shook Africa to its foundation the way Tutuola's has done. One day, and I wish it comes sooner, the Swedish Academy might begin to think seriously about awarding the Nobel Prize for literature to first-rate writers, and not to second-rate Peace fighters as they have done frequently. When that day comes, they should seriously consider Tutuola for the Nobel Prize for Literature. He merits it more than half-a-dozen winners I know. Why should we continue to honour Homer dead and deny the laurel to a Homer alive?

A word to our writers.

Writers are supposed to be the most sensitive (with heightened awareness) part of the community; where was the sensitivity of (for example) Nigerians when their country was heading for the maelstrom? Writers are supposed to be the seers; where was their prophetic eye when danger was all around? As prophets who can see the present more clearly, they should have interpreted the signs, signs big enough for the blind to see, before the blows fell. As prophets who can see the most distant event, couldn't they have seen beyond *A Man of the People?*

What were these writers doing except, with all the other boisterous Nigerians, enjoying the benefits of 'Nigeria the Example of Democracy in Africa'? What were they doing but despising the South African exile who they thought was so cowardly that he could not put up a fight but took to flight?

What were these writers doing except write songs of goats, toads for supper, write about blades! One of them was even a savage!

And the jackals cry: Tutuola is not relevant to modern Negeria! Who, among these writers, was relevant, or brave enough to be relevant? Only Cyprian Ekwensi on the popular level, and The Onitsha Market School on the lower popular level. Chinua Achebe was too late; he wasted his time offending the *chi* when he should have been grappling with the modern giant. Wole Soyinka is comprehensible in satires, less comprehensible in essays, and obscure in plays. Such an obscurity is the aspiration of every philosopher. Whatever message he wants to impart has difficulties passing through his thick masks. His histrionic abortive single-handed *coups* against the establishment are the mere tantrums of an *Antigone*.

The danger we face is not whether African literature is to be an appendage to African politics, and the politics of the government in power. If African literature is to be an appendage to anything, it had better be an appendage to literature — Eskimo literature, Papuan literature, any literature — so long as it is literature — rather than an appendage to politics. Literature and literature blend; literature and politics produce court artists and poor literature.

The source of our confusion is that the educated African grew up expecting a big man's post, replete with a car for elbow-out, a string of mistresses, quarters and everything that will make him the new bourgeois, living in comfort and amity with others of the same class. It seemed never to have entered our minds that some of us are going to find ourselves on different sides of the line, that some of us are going to be writers — poor, honest, heated critics of our government — because we love equality for everybody, and will fight for the rights of the unknown slum dweller or the landless one, or the servants of our very Ministers — and critics who will call a spade a spade, and call it aloud, loud enough to resound around the globe, and face detention camps.

We, who have begged for goat-skins and been given them, have to accept the tragic responsibilities which go with our calling. Tiresias did not fear Oedipus's big eyes. John the Baptist told the truth even if Herodias later had his head on a platter.

Let justice be done to all, and we shall be quiet; let a poor widow be wronged, then we shall fight till justice is done her. If we condone one injustice, there is no telling where that lion will strike next time.

What is Crocodile?

Dear Editor:

Mr. Sheldon G. Weeks's sentences on my article "Can We Correct Literary Barrenness In East Africa?" are interestingly illustrative of the difficulties of the literate. The latter part of his second paragraph is full of questions. The way he asks them would have made the jesting Pilate blush. And yet it is in those questions that he thinks his original contribution to discussion of East African literary barrenness is contained. Since writing (I mean serious writing) is an intellectual exercise, shall we conduct the discussion in a high key and at a high level?

Mr. Weeks tells me not to blame the British very much because I would have difficulties in explaining Nigeria's productivity. I confess I am no authority on Nigerian literature. Someone will have to do a comparative study of West and East African literary developments in order to enlighten us. Whenever such a work will be produced, I predict these factors will be high up on the list as contributory to Nigeria's superiority: traditions and superstitions control life more in West Africa than in East Africa.

Great arts have resulted from traditions and superstitions. Superstitions of course include beliefs not only in Juju, but also Mohammed and Allah, Jesus and God, Pope and Mary, Zeus, Jupiter and other organised myths and mythologies which are ingrained in cultures. It is because of these superstitions and traditions that Egyptian, Hebrew, Greek, Roman, Medieval, Renaissance arts flourished. For only a highly superstitious or imaginative (the two are cousins) mind writes *The Odyssey, The Aeneid, The Koran, The Divine Comedy, Paradise Lost* (to name only a few classics) for a superstitious audience. (If we still believe in them it only goes to show the power of superstitions.)

In West Africa superstition had already brought forth masks, bronze sculptures, and grand myths before the whites came. There had evolved traditions in art. The West African artists of today just made adjustments to the modern scene. Even in East Africa, among our highly superstitious and traditional tribes great works of art are coming forth. The Kikuyu among whom the Mau Mau could flourish gave us Ngugi, the first writer to produce a novel in English. Nagenda is a Muganda; the Baganda myths, superstitions, and traditions even now still force suited gentlemen to kneel before another mortal.

In South Africa, the tribe that produced Chaka has given us most of the prominent South African writers to be found in Nairobi and London. There is a great correlation between tradition, mythology and superstition on the one hand, and great art on the other. Those people from smaller tribes have difficulties making a mark.

In a sentence badly in need of reconstruction, Mr. Weeks thinks (evasively) that "perhaps" the blame really "lies with the occupational structure that developed and the aspirations of the people who though some could write they maybe saw no possible future as a writer (in terms of a living)?" After one has punctuated it and adjusted the agreements between nouns, pronouns, and articles, one turns to wonder as to what "occupational structure" could be claimed as having developed in the present East Africa in which a cowherd has turned a president and a "boy" bought his former "master's" shamba. As for "aspirations," some writers do not consider financial remuneration a great inducement. Even in East Africa, the late Swahili bard, Shaaban Roberts, hardly derived much financially from his works. It is the non-poet editors and anthologists who are reaping all the financial benefits from the writers' sweat.

And then when Mr. Weeks turns to the enumeration of the reasons which will lead to the development of our writers, he has so many possibilities that, had that literary dyke — the etc. — not been there, he would have gone on *ad infinitum*. The thing is, to be helpful, he should have come out with a few major reasons upon which he staked his honour. It requires intellectual courage to state things positively and not just to "raise questions". If we persist in dabbling in serious thinking, somewhere along the line, we shall have to do this. As it is, Mr. Weeks just gave us crude thoughts reflecting elementary stages in arriving at a solution. When Antony described the Nile crocodile: "It is shap'd sir, like itself; and it is as broad as it has breadth. It is just so high as it is, and moves with its organs"; we are bound to ask with Caesar: will this satisfy Lepidus? No.

Why will East African writers develop? I say for the same reasons that writers all over the world and in all ages have developed: to please a god (or God, whatever that may be), to please a king, or a president, or a nation, or a tribe, or a girl friend, or a boy friend, or the self; to criticise, abuse, teach, or correct misconceptions; to release emotion and ease frustration. In short, writers will be moved by love and hate. Even the timid and the shy, moved by joy or hurt have shown surprising ability at oratory. The love of God and the hatred of oppression have been some of the commitments which brought fame to people in the past.

Let us turn to a collateral reading of the first part of Week's letter and my article.

Count One. Mr. Weeks' claimed that I posed some answers to the question "why has East Africa lagged in the development of *its* writers" (italics mine). That would suggest that I was indicting East Africans for the barrenness. But my question (on page 8) was "why don't we have writers?" — quite a different thing from Mr. Weeks'.

Count Two. Mr. Weeks: "Contests like those of the East Africa Journal have been run in the past by the East African Literature Bureau ..." My article, (on page 12): "In fact I do not see the reason why the E.A.L.B. and Patel Press do not have magazines in which they could print writers' works. They could conduct competitions (I particularly refer to the Patel Press, since E.A.L.B. already organizes literary competitions ...") Where is the difference, apart from one being a paraphrase of the other?

Count Three. Mr. Weeks says that works received in E.A.L.B. competitions "have even been performed on the National Radio Works." I said (on page 12) that "We have had radio plays for years" and went on to suggest that great care should be taken on the scripts.

Count Four. Mr. Weeks says: "There are many budding writers such as Uganda's John Nagenda and Henry Kimbugwe." I wish for more! But actually

I did not miss John Nagenda. He is represented in David Cook's Makerere anthology. (On page 11) I said: "*Origin East Africa* is good as a beginning" and commented that, "It will have more meaning in history if those whose works appear there become prolific and advanced writers." (I am grateful to Mr. Weeks for the information on Henry Kimbugwe.)

Count Five. Mr. Weeks charges that I should have mentioned Gicaru's *Land of Sunshine*. I did not — but fine as that book is, I was not compiling a bibliographical article on East Africa. The genre and subject matter of *Land of Sunshine* is represented in the other works I cited.

Count Six. Mr. Weeks is intrigued with my having placed the blame for our literary barrenness on the British. He says that as if I was the first person he knows who ever blamed the British. Yet a certain gentleman argued aggressively against "British Export University". That gentleman even jumped on Makerere College for failure to produce literary men. Of a British English teacher he demands sarcastically, "Why have we had to wait until 1963 for the first East African novel?" The surprise is that this great critic of the British is our same Sheldon G. Weeks (see *Transition* 18 and 19).

Now if the university system was that poor, what about things beneath it? We were both criticising different aspects of the same thing. Perhaps Mr. Weeks has changed views? Anyway, I justified my charges by saying that, "Culturally, they stood aloof" and still maintain that we were being castrated culturally. I do not blame Mr. Weeks for not realizing the full extent of these things because only the real Africans who have suffered it can.

Count Seven. Mr. Weeks asks what he thought was the most devastating question, that the British "did serve as a reference group for shaping occupational aspirations but who embraced these models?" I pointed out (on page 9) that because the British were (and are) a practical minded people, "we became practical too ... (so we) ... debated and reasoned. This led directly to early writings which were of a quarrelsome nature; political grievances ..." I also pointed out, 'Poetry writing and the art of fiction were nòt taught" and therefore we had no "models" in these genres. The best our writers could do was to protest, for who could have written a Lugardesque treatise on "indirect rule" and called himself an East African? We did not have Royal Geographical Societies to report to; no Church Missionary Societies and, for that matter, no Fulbright grants for studies in Africa!

Count Eight. Mr. Weeks charges me most unfairly by saying, "It is interesting that most of the early 'explorers' and missionaries did write (including Lugard who does not fit Taban lo Liyong's stereotype.)"

I know the word 'stereotype' is very popular in most American circles, and therefore is liable to misuse. Weeks did just that. In my article (on page 7) I gave a long list of 'explorers' and missionaries: Baker, Stanley, Emin Pasha, Livingstone; others such as Conrad, Joyce Cary; still others like Karen Blixen and Huxley; and even paid tribute to Robert Ruark; and then (on page 9) I even mentioned not just one, but 'Lord Lugards'! Perhaps it is not Lugard who does not fit my 'stereotype', but Taban lo Liyong who does not fit Sheldon G. Weeks's stereotype!

A long exercise. But it helps with the psychological liberation. And, incidentally, this scrutiny forces me to

the conclusion that the Gentlemen from Harvard
Graduate School of Education, may be inflicted with fits
of a disease known as *illiteratus relapsus*.

Taban lo Liyong, Student
Howard University Washington,
D.C. U.S.A.

Weep Not, Child and Origin East Africa

East Africa is a land of variety. We have snow on Mount Kilimanjaro and sand in northern Kenya; the rift valley and the great lakes; the highlands and the plains; the farmers and the herders; the rich and the poor; the literates and the illiterates; the African tribes and Asian and European communities. These have been touched on by non-fiction writers, but the literary themes, situations, and characters they suggest are still searching for writers. The writing of poems and fiction in the English language is new here, and there is nothing to compare with the output in West Africa and South Africa. Thus, the few pioneering works so far produced in East Africa deserve close study.

Nigerian literature in English owes much to the University of Ibadan, from whence come such well-known writers as John Pepper Clark, Wole Soyinka, and Chinua Achebe. In East Africa, Makerere University College in Uganda is Ibadan's equivalent as the mother of the first generation of writers. Current and former students of this university have given us most of the trickle of literary works now available.

The first novel to come out of East Africa was James Ngugi's *Weep Not, Child,* written three years ago while the young Kenyan was reading English Honours at Makerere. He followed it up with another novel, *The River Between;* has published many short stories in *Pen-point,* the English Department journal which he edited; wrote a play, *The Black Hermit,* which was performed in The National Theatre, Kampala; and has contributed weekly political commentaries to Kenya's *Sunday Nation.*

Weep Not, Child is a story of Kenya during the Mau Mau Emergency period. Those bloody years are re-created through the experiences of three families — of Ngotho, a traditional Kikuyu; of Jacobo, a modernized Kikuyu who experiences the best and worst of his world and that of the white man; and Mr. Howlands, a white settler. They all love Kenya in their own ways but do not understand one another. Ngotho's son, Njoroge — hero of the story — travels through all three worlds and falls in love with Mwihaki, the daughter of his father's arch-enemy, Jacobo. Njoroge's brothers become Mau Maus, and subsequently kill Jacobo and Mr. Howlands and also cause the death of their father. In narrating the story, Ngugi gives us new insights into the various problems of Kenya at that time, including land, race, the Mau Mau freedom fighters, the 'traitors,' tribal suspicions, and difficulties of getting school fees.

If we consider the story on the analogical level, however, there is a deeper message. Ngugi is a disciple of Walt Whitman (from whose poem, 'On The Beach at Night,' comes the title of the novel). Ngugi believes in Whitman's concept of the brotherhood of man and remains optimistic that man can be improved. A second influence on Ngugi is obviously Dostoyevsky, whose chief characters in *The Brothers Karamazov* stand for distinct gradations of Russians — old Karamazov and his sinful sons belonging to the past, to a bygone period of Russian life, whereas Alyosha and his younger friends were looking to the future. In Ngugi's case, there are two groupings: the fathers and their sinful sons, mothers and their younger children. The fathers perish contesting the land they all love. Their older sons are sinful, hasty, and trigger-happy. Both Mr. Howlands and Ngotho lost a son each in World War II, and Ngotho produces more than his share of Mau Mau fighters. After killing the fathers, one of the sons is executed, another imprisoned for life, and a third held in a detention camp.

The mothers are symbolic of 'mother earth': they give and preserve life, and are wise. The women survive the emergency slaughter. The children are a new order, unstained by their parents' iniquities. They understand and love one another. Schooling contributes in dispelling the old myths and clearing away the suspicions which had kept their parents apart as well as engendering the new spirit of brotherhood among the children — Kenyans all — Nandi, Luo, Wakamba, Giriama, Kikuyu, stooges, patriots, blacks, whites, and Asians. That is why Njoroge loves Mwihaki and communicates with young Stephen Howlands, and why he was able to find in Siriana Secondary School that all Luo are not sorcerers. It soon becomes clear why the book is dedicated to Jasbir Kalsi, an Asian.

Most of the time Ngugi uses simple and short sentences. He has admirable figures of speech such as calling a chief "big" because he "used to eat with the Governor." There are others inappropriately used, however, such as use of the proverb "a lamb takes after her mother" to describe tigerish qualities. For comic relief, he gives us realistic classroom scenes. Ngugi is especially skilled in dramatizing the absurdity of the time when fate strikes. On the day when Mwihaki was jubilant over her success in school, she went home to find that her father had been mobbed. Njoroge had his brightest morning in school spoiled by being dragged to the "House of Pain" for interrogation for the murder of Jacobo.

The first few pages of *Weep Not, Child,* and some latter passages are reminiscent of Alan Paton's *Cry the Beloved Country.* When Njoroge identifies himself with David and the Kikuyu with the children of Israel, it is a poor imitation of Flaubert. Ngugi commits many technical sins, probably because he is more engrossed in exposing his ideas and ideals than in adhering to artistic precepts. The novel consists of too many unrelated essays and stories; things just do not dovetail. Then, too, Ngugi explains and summarizes situations which would lend themselves to easy dramatization. He rarely uses dialogue to help characterization. What is one who does not know the type to make of this: "In physical appearance at least, he [Mr. Howlands] was a typical Kenya settler"? We hear many more things than we see. For example, we can hear reports of guns, and the barber talking, and his scissors flicking away — but we never see the customer whose hair is being cut. Although traditional African sense of respect perhaps prohibits an author from "staring another in the face like a river snake," African writers must be as alert with their eyes, nose, and other senses, as they are with their ears. African writers must learn to use all their senses, as Alex la Guma does in *A Walk in The Night,* if they are to do full justice to their stories.

*   *   *

David Cook's anthology of writings by Makerere University College students introduces to us some new and inexperienced writers of obvious potential. The stories, plays, and poems compiled here are drawn from 17 editions of *Penpoint,* the journal of the English Department in the university. Of the 25 contributors, 20 come from Kenya, Tanzania, and Uganda; there are also two Malawians, one Nigerian, two Americans, and one who is British. Some of these contributors are still doing their undergraduate studies in Makerere; others have gone to do graduate studies in other universities; and some of them are already holding responsible posts.

The editor does not define what he regards as "East African literature." If he had adhered to the academic definition of African literature — "Creative writing in which an African setting is authentically handled or to which experiences originating in Africa are integral" — some of the best works in the volume would have been disqualified because they are written by Americans. Fortunately, David Cook recognized the cosmopolitan and international character of Makerere, and gave us works written in East Africa.

The editor takes care to point out that these writings come from "original course work undertaken as part of the study of style," thus precluding the inevitable criticism of the East African short story as being "anecdotal" and "explanatory." In fact, few of the short stories in this volume are worthy of the name. Technically, the

short story is not a story which is merely short;
it is a brief narrative which has unity, compression,
originality in the plot, point of view, outcome or character,
and ingenuity. Among these writers, more emphasis should
now be laid on the techniques of short story writing rather
than on style. The book also suffers from one editorial
oversight: the dates when these writings first appeared
in *Penpoint* are not given. Thus, we have no way of
assesing the development of facility in English in the
university since *Penpoint* was born in 1958, and we cannot
follow the development of those students who have more
than one contribution.

Most of the contributions in the Cook collection fall
into the categories of "an incident which took place in my
village" or "story my grandmother once told me."
Some deal with clashes between tradition and superstition
on the one hand and Christianity and modern
pragmatism on the other. But when these writers deal
with the passing of the old ways, they do not adopt
the sentimentality and nostalgia so characteristic of the
negritude school. Joe Mutiga remembers ceremonial days
when "the Akikuyu were a tribe" instead of "part of a
nation," and is sure "it is happier thus in all." David
Rubadiri's poem, "Stanley Meets Mutesa," reenacts those
first moments of the black/white encounter from which
present-day Africa derives.

James Ngugi, who helped with the compilation of
the anthology, is represented by four stories. "The Fig
Tree" treats of a barren woman who must cross a river
to seek out the god of fertility under the Mukuyu tree
in the land of ghosts. Her adventure is sufficiently dramatic
to make one think of a master like Flaubert; but his story
cannot be fully understood unless one has a copy of an

as-yet-unwritten encyclopedia of Kikuyu myths. Another writer who presents somewhat the same problem is Jonathan Kariara, who contributes a touching bit of tragedy in "Unto Us a Child Is Born."

G. K. Gicogo's "Sound of Njeru" is a folktale retooled into a short story with plot, suspense, and all. "And This, at Last," by John Nagenda, has mystery, horror, and psychology, giving it a distinct flavour. Although Tilak Banerjee's "An Orissan Love Story" is written in prose, it is really poetry, as lyrical and fragile as Keats', and as tragic as a Greek drama. Banerjee's Asian origin is evident in the theme and its treatment, and his story suggests one of the ways by which Asian cultures enrich East African culture. "The Talisman" by McCarthy develops too slowly, but the plot is good and the execution better than most in this volume.

From the technical point of view, "A Prescription," by N. G. Ngulukulu, is excellent. This restrained story has the conflicts, flashbacks, involvements, subtlety, and realism absent in the others. The recounting of a meal hosted by the protagonist includes a beautiful description of a process that I have participated in thousands of times without realizing its literary potential: "What each one of the guests had to do to allay his hunger was merely to take part of the solid stuff from the plate, roll it into a ball, press the thumb into it to make a small hole, dip it in the sauce and convey the mixture into his mouth."

Among the plays, "Ladipo's Last Stand," by Tunde Aiyebusi, possesses a serious theme, strong plot, development, and suspense. These qualities help to offset Aiyebusi's ineptitude in pulling characters onto the stage and pushing them off so awkwardly, and his tendency to have everybody forever shouting. His theme, a most appropriate one, is that we have to pay for progress toward modernity by parting with some things we have long cherished.

John Bing, an American, contributes a surrealistic play called "The Wall," which contends that walls, far from protecting us, preserve our fears, prejudices, and ignorances; they are built because of suspicions and perpetuate misunderstandings. Peter Nazareth deals lightly with the "other side" of a Makerere student's life in an amusing play, "Brave New Cosmos." Kaggwa, an undergraduate, has a practical reason for reading English: the acquisition of apt quotations to be employed in borrowing money from friends. He will not repay a loan because Shakespeare's Polonius advised him as long ago as 1601 that: *Neither a borrower, nor a lender be; For loan oft loses both itself and friend.*

All said, *Origin East Africa* introduces to us some writers whom we are likely to hear from again if they survive the critics' "hazing," get further professional assistance, and are willing to work at honing their evident talents.

Negritude: crying over split milk

If a man cries over spilt milk, he must be either a fool who does not know how to milk, or an ignoramus who does not know what a cow is, or does not know how and where else more milk could be obtained, or has not yet learnt that there is such a thing as synthetic milk, or is not aware that he could do without milk altogether.

We hear that Negritude is a search, a search for a past, a lost past. Something that is lost, like last year, for example, is lost. You might join the proverbial dog and bay at the moon if you want its return. Of the two varieties of romantics — those who dream ahead and those who languish in the remembrance of times past — I would rather dream ahead and model utopias, erewhons. A stronger will would seize both horns of the dilemma, confront it, grapple with it, now. After all, yesterday's people began their day yesterday, we begin ours today: by facing the realities that are here now. Marx said religion is the opium of the people chiefly, I think, because it robs us of living in this life and encourages us to grow long necks, giraffe-like, evolution-wise, for peeping into heaven. Nietzsche did not say (or did he?) that it is as useless to simulate a hangover.

Now that time and winds of change have heaped cultures upon cultures upon the so-called golden age — Negritude — how are you going to bore a way down to that cherished time? Perhaps one goes in through Leo Frobenius' anthropological passage singing: "The African way of thought is different from everybody else's." A person knows, that is all right with him, he also wants to be thought different (and why not? isn't the whole idea of writing an attempt to express one's difference?) but, and this is the point, scout Frobenius found he was wrong. And what is more, he recanted. What is going to happen to those who grab at anything which offers immediate, albeit momentary, support? Leopold Sedar Senghor states: "The African is as it were shut up inside his black skin. He lives in primordial night. He does not begin by distinguishing himself from the object, the tree or stone, the man or animal or social event. ... He does not analyse it." By what means then did he arrive at the conclusion that the Western way of life was not good for him? And the European? He is "an objective intelligence, a man of will, a warrior, a bird of prey, a steady gaze. He first distinguishes the object from himself. He keeps it at a distance ... With his precision instruments he dissects it in a pitiless — factual analysis." Some Germans, perhaps. Latins too, *monsieur*? Following from that, possibly, pop poet LeRoi Jones says that jazz is a Negro speciality: constitutional. Whites don't "dig" it. Fair enough. Let's read the writing on the other side of that coin: "Classics are understood by whites only; Negroes don't dig them." How do you like that? Have there never been varieties of arrogance like that for most of the time, and to people like LeRoi Jones' disadvantage? Perhaps they would not be writing the type of things they write if it had not been for Jim Crow. Let's settle for this: Music is an art governed by its own laws, master those laws and you can be a good white Duke Ellington or a black Maria Callas.

Perhaps again, Father Placide Tempels' *Bantu Philosophy* might be your base for fashioning an African philosophy. But then, remember: although Bantus are in Africa, not all Africans are Bantu. Father's study is superficial and unscientific; inspired, perhaps. Then one might call upon the assistance of erudite German scholarship. Nobody beats Germans in thorough, painstaking research. But when it gets to *Muntu,* an attempt to justify the ways of the lost generation to youth, you begin to wonder why Herr Jahn did not exert his energy in more worthwhile endeavours. Perhaps he might now decamp and head towards Red China; it is there that the battle to rid the land of all Western influences is raging with the vigour of the dragon. To a German mind, dictatorship is quite in order. But nobody yet knows the mind of Africa (Professor Abraham, excuse me) ; African socialism, although there are commendable efforts by all sorts of bodies; African literature, a subject not much explored yet because of scantiness of material, although, as an adjunct to the study of African politics from the point of view of those who are all out for domination, it yields grants for study abroad or special studies of unspecified kinds.

Who has the audacity to face me and theorise about *the* African mind or literature, etc.? The best that can be done is to dissect a small island, like Haiti, for example, and come up with the answer that its culture is dominantly African, as Dr. J. Price-Mars did. Up till now I had been taught that a lot of observations, research, findings are done before a student could arrive at a theory. But I understand Africa is a special case; it can be by-passed by all time-honoured scientific methods and yet the theorist arrives at perfectly scientific conclusions.

The white man is very humanitarian. If anyone doubts it, he should see how he saved the Red Indian from possible extinction from overwork, at the hands of considerate American colonists. That priest who had compassion for the Red Indians had the originality to suggest African replacement (the load is always there; you may shift the weight to the left and later to the right, but put it down you can't) — because the African is a hardier beast of burden. (Negritudists' special qualities were observed that long ago!) Those slaves who managed to cross the Atlantic were dispersed: children from parents, one tribesman from another, friend from friend. And their Americanisation continued, including the slaves mating with their masters and masters' sons. There — in the barns, beds (if conditions were favourable or control difficult), shack, bush — Europe met Africa. What do we say, do we say the issues were African (African descent?) or European (European descent?) This is a very important point. To call them of African descent is to fail in point of fact. The Negro is a EurAfrican in America although through the ages the white man in his generosity has forgotten his share in the project. When we begin to split hairs (kinky ones, too) we will have to admit that the American Negro is both a cultural and racial mixture. Culturally (jazz excepted and included) he is mostly European and American; racially, there are more darker Negroes (dominant genes? a fact for Negritudists), but there are also some white Negroes, hence the qualification: James Meredith is the first *known* Negro to be enrolled in the

University of Mississippi. If some of these Negroes could feel some racial and cultural identities with their African ancestors, others of them are equally justified in feeling the same for whites who make up the other part of the heritage. Also American whites are a very different breed of whites from those of, say, the Scandinavian countries. They are whites whose ways of life are influenced by the Negro presence. But let a Negro as much as stretch his hand to help a white and the shouted derision of Uncle Tom would din our ears.

Are the American Negro and the African, the same thing? No, not yet. The solidarity of the dark peoples of the world is quite a good thing in politics, if all the coloured people can use it always to their advantage. But as I see it now it is very likely to harm the Africans, since bigger powers can make use of it to their advantage. The old world philosophy of "kith and kin" (essentially Anglo-Saxon: the French do not have an appropriate word for it, hence the idea defeated them in Indo-China and Algeria) — kith and kinness never settles a political issue permanently, or as permanently as political solutions could. Let Africans adopt a kith and kinness with American Negroes and they will discover that the "Star Spangled Banner" can be served and spread through Duke Ellington's jazz, Langston Hughes' poetry, Mercer Cook's French, leave alone that brave boy who braved Ghanaian ire to rescue the U.S. flag from being torn up.

Africans don't have long spoons yet, therefore, let us sup at a distance. Perhaps Sekou Toure was wise after all in not sending Guineans to participate in Senghor's Folly called the First World Festival of Negro Arts. Who can tell where the wolf comes from? Especially now that he comes dressed in University gowns. The magazine

Ramparts says be careful, especially with the products of Michigan State University. But they actually come from everywhere, in all sizes and shapes, guises and colours, ranks and types of visa. Be vigilant. Negritude and non-alignment cannot co-exist.

The white man had maintained that Africans and Negroes have no past (although the Negro's other past is very well known to them) and therefore have no future. The idea that you need a past in order to have a future, like a building whose deep foundation supports the upward mass, strikes me as being silly: I mean for men. Negritudists accepted it and by a peculiar process which only a French trained mind is capable of, converted their ignorance and poverty into strength. Let Aime Cesaire say it himself:

> Glory to those who invented neither powder nor the compass
> Those who tamed neither gas nor electricity
> Those who have explored neither the seas nor the skies.

— So what? When anybody decides to answer a silly question, the answer is likely to turn out silly. Among the white men, only a few have been inventors. The rest of them cannot even write poetry. Talk about discovering the seas, one of the Negroes went right to the pole. But even another Negritudist went on to prove that Western culture is founded on African culture borrowed from Egypt by Greece, from Greece by Rome, then spread all over the world to be upheld by such likely and unlikely people as Queen Elizabeth (both ladies qualify), President Johnson, General de Gaulle, Rebel Smith, Prime Minister Verwoerd (he was slain while I was writing this; I found no good reason for leaving his name out), and all the red necks. Cheikh Anta Diop, your *Nations negroes et cultures* is quite an exercise. Perhaps we, the young, should now turn to proving what we can do rather than what our ancestors did.

Oliver Goldsmith, in his "The Deserted Village," sings some very modern lines:

> While thus the land adorned for pleasure
>> all
> In barren splendour feebly waits the fall.
> E'en now the devastation is begun.
> And half the business of destruction done;
> E'en now, methinks as pondering here I stand,
> I see the rural virtues leave the land.

That was when industrialization was coming into England; that is now when five-year plans are devised by Ministers of Economic Planning (and may they give us enough maize and matoke and rice) from Dakar to Dar es Salaam. Senghor knows (he should) very well that industrialization is progress (not necessarily moral progress, I also take it, but morals are appendixes to the politico-economic conditions of the world), is inevitable, and comes to destroy the rural virtues of simplicities. But he cannot lead Senegal into the twentieth century without industrialization and destruction of that rural innocence (the name sounds sublime enough to merit a painting by William Blake or another by Albrecht Durer called 'Nostalgia'). A poet-politician, how much trust should we have in him? Perhaps he needs a psychiatrist to iron out his schizophrenia every night in the poem.

Goldsmith's son in the poem, Luke, for a time sent home "the prettiest letters that were ever seen." But after many months, he slackened in writing and "at length,/ He in the dissolute city gave himself/To evil courses," and

193

then ignominy and shame fell on him. — At least he could still realize that his integrity was shattered.

What, with all that industrialization, detribalization, desecration, desegregation, miscegenation, and education, befoggation; whose mind could be expected to steer the narrow path always? Especially now that morals are as elusive as ephemeral, codes of behaviour are in flux? Pittsburgs, Birminghams, Southamptons are planted, discovery of Lorraine valleys, where Congo tropical forests once stood are made by us; yet the employment and neurosis arising therefrom, the frustrations, strikes and unemployments, the social disorganization... Here is no golden age, no room for Voltaire's noble savage, or Henri Rousseau's setting for his paintings which are actually patterns of leaves. Your commonwealth should not resemble Gonzalo's, its end forgetting the beginning. Michael Dei-Anang, the Ghanian poet, had clarity of vision to proclaim (in the Era of the Redeemer) that:

> Here we stand
> Poised between two civilizations
> Backwards? (NEVER!) To days of drum
> And festal dances in the shade
> Of sun-kist palms.
> Or forward? (ALWAYS.)
> Forward!
> Toward?

Anything, slums included. When you move forward, the rotation of the world carries you along, increasing your speed exceedingly. Try standing still, or worse, going back and you will cry like Julius Caesar: "Help me, Cassius, or I sink!"

Perhaps students should fear dropping out of school more than going to hell. Lucky (really) are they who are born with silver spoons in their mouths, or who learnt to declaim by the seaside with pebbles in their mouths, or who are physically strong enough to join the military. Woe unto the villager — he who goes to Lagos city with much energy, perhaps some money, a vote, and less wit. If he still has some wits left when he returns, let's hear his tales of trickery and robbery. I am concerned about the ordinary man, so are you.

> Black woman
> Naked woman, black woman
> Clothed with your colour which is life,
> with your form which is beauty!
> In your shadow I have grown up: ...

But only in your 'shadow.' The marriage of black man to white woman has been going on, literally and symbolically. Even Senghor who wrote that praise (an afterthought?) knows it, if anybody does. Now what song will the white sons of black Negritudists sing? Or taking the highbrow judgement that a literary school provides a free-for-all, what inspiration does Negritude hold for a Frenchman, a Chinese, or an Eskimo? Re-affirmation of racism?

There is a mass of educated ignorance surrounding the Africans. At one time they were taken for the cousins-germane of the monkeys (Darwin misunderstood? But even Huxley, his bulldog, could not go the whole urang), and later, as Negritudists will tell you, our cultures were trampled down (Social Darwinism). With those, and others, is it strange that the bile, the glandular and nonglandular secretion inside Aime Cesaire were so stirred up that he had to fume:

195

"... for centuries Europe has stuffed us with lies and bloated us with pestilence ..." and, gathering momentum, he went on:

"And this country cried for centuries
that we were stupid brutes; that
the pulsations of humanity stopped before the doors,
of niggerness; that we are a walking dunghill, hideously
promising sweet sugarcanes and silky cotton, and
they branded us with red-hot irons and we slept in
our excrements and they sold us on the market for
less than an ell of English cloth or some
salted Irish meat, and this country was calm, tranquil,
and was convinced that it acted in accordance with
the will of God."

Give me a lever and where to stand and I will push the world, cried the blind thinkers of old. Now here are all the lever, fulcrum, and where to stand. It is steams like the above which have been keeping the world moving, changing. A man — not a poet, poets are wrongheaded, the energy they should have exerted against the world they pack into a few lines on pages — a man would have done something concrete instead of defending, rebutting, explaining, justifying, equivocating...

Oh, Matthew Arnold. You said what the literature of power is. You did not live long enough to say that Negritude is the literature of weakness. It is. Maintain the literature and you perpetuate the weakness. But even the king of kings, Osymandyas, after saying: "Look on my works, ye Mighty, and despair!" could not live even in stone — nothing of his statue remained but "a shapeless rock of granite." Nothing remains but change.

Ban, Ban, Caliban. What did Prospero teach Caliban? Language. What did Caliban do with it? Curse. A curse is a compressed prose, to be hurled against one's enemy like a hand grenade. And language itself is the forged currency of communication. Beware of falling in love with the currency rather than the article of trade. There are things you must do but not name. Name them, they die. That's what happened to Negritude.

In one of Prospero's books is written:

> Time, place, and manners do I seek, and these
> Are found in plenteous store of our past.

That became the Negritude hobbyhorse — the collecting, numbering, and dusting of old philosophies, arts, culture, juju, voodoo. It was also the rite of purification, purification from contamination with Western ways, in preparation for a re-entry into the tribal life.

Dennis Osadebay wanted just one thing: his "affairs themselves sort us." He had this plea, and he is not in the Negritude camp:

> Don't preserve my customs
> As some curios
> To suit some white historian's tastes.

If he had written now, he would have found some difficulty in classification. How would he differentiate from historians Central Intelligence Agency wolves who masquerade as scholars and specialists? — they are specialists all right, but of sorts. Mr. Osadebay should know that some Africans have new tastes.

The concern with cultural rebirth was quite legitimate. After all, says Senghor, France "invites me to her table and bids me bring my bread, ... gives with the right hand and takes away half with the left." But, apart from patching grief with proverbs, (quite an irrelevant occupation for anybody who wants to move ahead), in terms of modern world, what can Negritude's uncertain past yield? Nobody would have quarrelled with Christopher Marlowe's "Passionate Shepherd's song to his Love:"

> Come live with me and be my Love,
> And we will all the pleasures prove.
> That hills and valleys, dales and fields.
> Or woods or steepy mountain yields.

If Sir Walter Raleigh's Nymph had not replied wisely thus:

> If all the world and love were young,
> And truth in every shepherd's tongue,
> These pretty pleasures might me move,
> To live with these and be thy love.
> But time drives flocks from field to fold,
> When rivers rage, and rocks grow cold;
> And Philomel becometh dump;
> The rest complains of cares to come.

To take the First World Festival of Negro Arts as the triumph, glorification, and vindication of Negritude, rather than its twilight, is to be narrow-minded. How restrictive can any philosophy be if it is to be applied only to the African continent, leave alone North America, the Caribbean Islands, and South America? Isn't that going to omit the sons (and daughters) of Negritude? Whatever programme may be needed for the people, the individual has his own plans also. A few individuals will not surrender their own cherished programmes for anyone else's, life or death. No doubt some of us are romanticists, but others are realists, impressionists, expressionists, arts for art's sakists, nothingists, everythingists. Even in Russia where literature is controlled they are having a hard time herding the poets. Inward looking philosophy suffocates.

It is true that Negroes and Africans have been so good as to be honoured with the Nobel Peace Prize. Ralph Bunche gathered one — he gave the sons of Israel a homeland. Chief Albert Luthuli was given one, although his children are still in bondage. Martin Luther King got one but Governor Wallace is still in full control of Alabama. This is not because we are the monopolists of non-violence, though. But Julian Bond who does not want to go to fight in Viet Nam had this apt remark to make:

> Look at that gal shake that thing
> We cannot all be Martin Luther King.

We are not all ascetics; some of us do not want to go to nunneries and monasteries. We do not want to darken heaven, either; some of us will take our respective places in hell. But right now, most of us want to live a satisfying life between earth and sky. Non-violence, or educated cowardice, we leave to the few. If we are hungry we steal, if we are opposed, we fight our way in and out. Satisfaction is what we want.

Lord Byron pointed to the heart of the matter:

Afric is...

...full of power
For good or evil.

And, as if elaborating on that and giving it other dimensions, Ezekiel Mphahlele (who alone saw the wheel, now thought to have been an Unidentified Flying Object) said this, worthy of serious thoughts by African leaders as well as Negritudists:

> "What I do not accept is the way in which too much of the poetry inspired by Negritude romanticises Africa — as a symbol of innocence; purity and artless

primitiveness. I feel insulted when some people imply that Africa is not also a violent continent. I am a violent person, and proud of it because it is often a healthy human state of mind; some day I am going to plunder, rape, set things on fire; I'm going to cut someone's throat; I'm going to subvert a government; I'm going to oppress my own people; I'm going to hunt down the fat black men and destroy them; I'm going to become a capitalist, and woe to all who cross my path; I'm going to lead a breakaway church — there's money in it; I'm going to attack the black bourgeoisie while I cultivate a garden, rear dogs and parrots, listen to jazz and classics; yes I'm going to organize a strike. Don't you know that sometimes I kill to the rhythm of drums and cut the sinews of a baby to cure it of paralysis? ... this is only a dramatization of what Africa can do and is doing. The image of Africa consists of all these things and others. And Negritude poetry pretends that they do not constitute the image and leaves them out."

That is my centrepiece. I have always wanted to produce such a classic but found that somebody has said it before.

The deputies *d'outre-mer*, briefs in hand, went to the metropole where they were more at home. They came and were promised everything, and took it literally. But there are built-in mechanisms which bar blacks at certain gates. Frankly, the Western way was not fashioned with the idea that the black man would be treated as an equal. It is undergoing the crisis of accommodating and being accommodated. When the black Frenchmen discovered there were limitations to their Frenchness, they turned foxes and said: French culture is bad anyway. Sour-grapes. In turning away from that pursuit and going back to accept their former ways, *they in effect discovered their own better reasons why they should have been discriminated against in the first place.* They christened what the French had called vices, virtues. Yet they did not leave the scene completely like Aesop's fox; they went on helping themselves to the fallen fruits secretly as well as receiving from the hand of the gardener.

Whether Africa invented or did not invent powder, steam, compass or electricity is not the issue now. What we know is that *Africa must use powder, steam, compass and electricity,* now. How we get these depends on our means.

Past backwardness should not be congealed into a philosophy when conditions are changing rapidly. Unless one maintains the status quo in order to prove his point. To embrace Negritude is to shackle mind, to be tethered to proved myths, religions and superstitions; it means to be inhibited and confined; it calls for respect for old useless ways, and that means fear. What we need is more irreverence so that this golden opportunity, when everything is in chaos after the destruction of the old colonial regimes, is used to push the freedom of man and mind to its utmost limit. When I say this I do not only have Africa in mind but the whole world, all cultures.

Past cultures were developed because of religious and political reasons, when religions had real meanings in the lives of people. Now we have motivations somewhat different from those. How can we be expected to produce works of art according to the old styles when we do not have identities of outlook to life? If those voluptuous sculptures, carvings, were made to appease sensual gods; if those weird masks were projections of ideas of vengeful and capricious spirits; if music and poetry were for supplicating and softening the hard hearts of deities; if all this time this was done under fears and delusions, what becomes of art after enlightenment?

If in the Dark Ages one did not know whether one lived in hell, earth or heaven; if all paintings, writings plays, sculptures, were done for the delight of those delinquent spirits who fertilized their own mothers and were then reborn; supposing you were commissioned by pope or doge or king or president; if you praised a hero, how do you expect your youngsters to produce similar works of art when these cherished idols, myths, heroes and heroines have lost their inspiring quality? In a Godless age (Nietzsche witnessed His death), age of immoral wars and little patriotism, age of selfishness, there is no agreed yardstick, no agreed form, nothing is *de rigeur*, art included. That is why Negritude is disqualified.

We must have an abundance of curiosity — fortunately, curiosity kills cats only. That curiosity will enable us to search for and choose what is good for our coverings, stomachs, and intellects. If one of us finds his literary ancestor in China, well and good, let him give us poetry according to the ancient wise Chinese; if the songs of David inspire another, let him enrich our literature with modern psalms, we need psalms anyway in order to count our blessings; if some of us would like to compose symphonies after Mozart, they should not be stopped, there are already too many players of listeners' favourites; if some of our writers and artists would like to work from islands in the Pacific, let them go, Robert Louis Stevenson, Paul Gauguin, and others have been there before; if we have a Homer or a Virgil, let him sing the origin of the tribe; if some of our scientists would like to fly to the moon, let them take up American or Russian citizenship and go. As it is, we have too many people doing what they are not suited for anyway because of lack of opportunities in our part of the twentieth century. If some of us would like to settle in England and perhaps set that country towards becoming a coloured country, give them passports, let them go, there is wisdom in letting the disgruntled go where they want to, ask Fidel Castro; if some of us would like to run let them ask Keino how he does it, and those who enjoy bloodying peoples' noses should ask Champ Clay Elijah Mohammed, and, with good feeding and training, the Olympic Games could be dominated by the dark peoples of the world (including the game of sex, which I understand is the major reason for segregation in Southern United States). The world is still very young. All possible experiments have not yet been done. We must accept changes and produce changes.

Sometimes Senghor says wise things, non-Negritude things. This is one of them:

"I think all the great civilizations ... result from an interbreeding ... In my opinion, and objectively, this interbreeding is necessary. It is a result of the contact between civilizations. Indeed, either the external situation has changed and cultural borrowing enables us to adapt ourselves to the new situation, or the external situation, has not changed, and cultural borrowing enables us to better adaptation to the situation."

This is French circumlocution. In English precis, Senghor means: cultural borrowing is good. And that, unfortunately for Senghor, kills Negritude. He says Negritude is concerned mostly with the way things are said: the whining of the blues and Spirituals, the rhythm of feet on the ground, rather than the message. But some

203

Africans, through borrowing perhaps, or inclination, or constitution, are more concerned with the message than the methods. Jean-Paul Sartre claims Negritude is the being-in the world of the Negro. Is it a static being in-the-world, or as we would expect, a changing one? Whether we welcome it or not, cultural givings and takings are going ahead.

Contemporary African politicians are rebels, Liberia excluded. They wrenched power from the colonial masters. Where this process was hard, the nationalists had to raise political temper to a threatening height before independence could be granted. And that is the problem — the height of political consciousness, rebellion against a poor regime, an unjust regime, a regime that cannot provide most things people yearn for. Independence has been attained, but the spirit of rebellion is still active. Perhaps towards the granting of independence our politicians should have embarked on teaching us life in the new state, the realities of life in young nations. This was not done anywhere. Senghor now lives in a glass house. But he had written this against the French colonial masters, that they had turned his "household servants into 'boys', my peasants into wage-earners, my people into a working class ..." And then later he wore those French shoes. He never wrote a poem to explain to his people that even in utopia workers are essential. And he is a philosopher-king!

It is a most difficult thing to control the destiny of a young nation. The people's expectations are many and high, thanks to those wise politicians who promised things as if they had King Midas' power of alchemy: the wherewithal to satisfy these expectations is scarce; the diversion of attention of the poor, hungry, envious and alert is difficult (especially if they can see visible signs of affluence of their erstwhile poor neighbours now cruising in Mercedes Benzes) ; the suppression of gadflies (also known as 'trouble-makers') is hard: the general feeling is there and the removal of one spokesman does not take it away. Now, what is a politician to do? Nobody knows; I don't. Probably that is one of the reasons why I will remain a pedestrian all my life. ("Awake, my St. John! Leave all meaner things/To low ambition, and the pride of kings.") Africa is ripe for revolutions and the leaders must revolutionize things. (Flashback: Mphahlele in depth, some pages back.) In this world of increased mass communication, minds can no longer be tethered. Magis are returning from pilgrimages (performed in mind or body) and are remarking:

> We returned to our places, these Kingdoms,
> But no longer at ease here, in the old
>   dispensation . . .

The past Magis (Senghor included) rid their countries of the "alien people". And that is where Negritude did a good job: in politics. Negritude is a useful tool, like the Osagyefo's (and he is still Osagyefo to me, he did more for the black man than Jesus) , African Personality.

Writing of Aime Cesaire, Andre Breton had this to say, and what he says here should be applied to all Negritude poets and other fighters for independence: "Experience indicates that . . . it is upon the poets that the charge has been laid to cut the iron braces that strangle us, and it is noteworthy that posterity tends to consecrate only whose who have contributed most to this task."

There are many "iron braces that strangle us" and attempts are always being made to fashion more by those in power: black, white, yellow. But more "poets" are also being born. The old have done their tasks under the banner of Negritude. Younger ones will have to continue the struggle to better the human condition after their parent's good efforts, and in most cases, mistakes. Ultimately, a new order characterized by individualism — each individual chasing his own satisfaction, or running away from threats from another individual or an impersonal source — will be the best for man. We have been fighting group fights and never really known what we have been fighting for or why; sufficient were the leader's explanations or orders.

African culture is to be a synthesis and a metamorphosis — the order of things to come. It assimilates and it disseminates. It picks, it grabs, it carries on. It modifies, it combines — it does everything designated by the words active, changing and progress. As Cesaire has said, Negritude set aside: "the work of man has only begun," and "it remains for man to conquer all prohibitions immobilized in the corner of his fervour" and *"no race has a monopoly of beauty, intelligence, strength and there is room for all in the rendezvous of conquest ..."* (Italics ours.) This is the crossroad and cross-breeding place. No mules are born. Trespassers will not be prosecuted. Indeed, New York (and Paris, and Moscow, and Peking) "let the black blood flow into your blood"; let it flow uncontrolled. A racially and culturally mixed person is the universal man; all is in him; he identifies with all; he is kith and kin to all other Homo sapiens. This leads us to a super-Brazil. He will have slant eyes, kinky hair, Roman nose, Red Indian knight-errantry, democratic folly, dictatorial changeability, Maori tattoos, use English as a tool for rebuilding Babel Tower. All these (and more) will make him the hundred per cent African; the descendant of Zinjanthropus, the culturally and racially mixed man of the future.

Postscript

Dear Leonard,

By the way, let them keep Chaucer at Makerere, by all means. And Boccaccio too. And *Beowulf*. *The Golden Ass*. *Theogony*. *The Upanishad*. *Annalects* of Budha the Compassionate. *The Bible*, yes, the Bible too! And why not? *The Koran* has to find a place. Cervantes, by all means. + Ngugi now.   + Kibera tomorrow.

Frankly, it is not yet worth it. The establishment of a Chair of African Literature is not yet worth all the effort. Regardless of those already established.

There is African literature, yes. But how much? There's the snag. Yes, we have our myths. But who has done an extensive or definitive research in them yet? Or who has used them as literary springboards? We have traditional African literature. But how many traditionals do we have? We have a few stories, and novels, and poems. But who has shifted through the quantity to arrive at quality? Isn't it rather that now any African who gets published is *an* African writer, meaning a *GREAT* writer? What about critics? Critics to guide our tastes and choices? In tantrum, we have doubted or repulsed non-us critics and have not demonstrated an ability to do anything, leave alone that of real merit. I am an African and because of that I wish we would wait for five or more years before we begin to think of a Chair of African Literature in earnest. Meanwhile, African Literature should feel happy, should have no grudge, being taught as a subject, (one of the subjects) in the Comparative Literature Departments, where such departments exist, or in the English Departments.

Whatever you do keep Chaucer. Africa must be able to absorb all, contain all there was, all there is, all there will be. And administrators must be, or become, or remain visionaries who have the courage to have the integrity to direct, yes, they must be directors, using their best judgements as guides. When the days of stock-taking come, we shall be disturbed, nay, we shall regret, how many *human* things we have cast to the winds in the name of nationalism, Africanism, Negritude. We have gone on amputating some just human sides of Man-in-Africa in pursuit of mind control that we have left him maimed, thwarted, restless without knowing the cause, inadequate to function in a multisided world, circumscribed him in a cage of our making (unwitting designers). If the world was still compartmentalised, and communications from outside could be sealed off completely, we would be almost sure of the worth of out circumscription; if all the world were going our way, we could plead that we were not alone; if we could be left alone we would have swollen indeed with our greatness and humanism; if all the world was filled with doves we would surely fly together. The world is expanding; we are contracting. Circumscribed, we are that tiny (mental dwarfs, empty tins), that simple, that naive ... when we close our eyes with our hands we think, like children, that others cannot see us. What is needed from Africa is

Homo Complexus with *Nexuses* to everything there is or has been done or will be done by *Home Sapiens* the world over.

One who has a long journey (a world journey) to make must be able to take everything African in his stride while marching vigorously ahead (for me African literature is just a hobby, something I have done on the side). Leave petty slogans to KANU, UPC, KPU, TANU, and the whole gangs of them (crooks, deceits, hypocrites, yes, intellectual hypocrites, yes, intellectual usurpers — why are they usurpers? because intellectuals, true intellectuals have not yet arisen) the world over. Undercut them by constructing a solid intellectual brick today, Tomorrow, another. Next week, lay a foundation, accumulate a treasure, a mine, build a monument that will last, that will draw more attention than a politician's birth place, or a politician's seaside resort, or a politician's foundation.

Look at it this way: somewhere in America, somewhere in Britain, somewhere in Germany, somewhere in Australia, somewhere in France there is a boy or a girl of the same age with you, in the same year in university with you (literary history has evidences of writers who did wonders when they were your age or younger, or who were less educated than you are) and these students we are imagining are perhaps writing the classics of the future. Why not you also? In deed, why not?

In any case, what is there so sacred about things African? (Oh, Noliwe!) One ought to become a cynic, a Cynic, in order to rise above everything, in order to gain a vantage point, in order to see everything on a par. On par, they are all diversions, useless endeavours, endeavours whose absolute use is the means of channelling energy, and whiling away time while one is still in the state of conscious chemico-biologico-physiological functioning. Transcendentalised a Cynic, one surveys all as a vast panorama where games have been played, are being played, and will be played by dogs and worms, and cabbages and drosophila. One can't shed tears over anything: Viet Nam, Sharpeville, Pinto, African Socialism, etc., etc., *ad infinitum et ad absurdum*. What one can shed, and shed superfluously are crocodile tears. Just to make use of the tear glands, if one has forgotten to mock with tears. Any time one gets indignant, it is in mock indignation, or used for intellectual exercise. Just to display one's intellectual virtuosity. And absolutely nothing more up or below. Activate one's intellect, display one's intellectual muscles in the Olympics, in pentathlon, in decathlon. Create puzzles for others; give occupation to teachers and rulers; give headaches to the students who will have to try to match their intellects with one's records. It is clearly an act of impudence, something one does not believe in, or that has no value above the *doing,* something one does not moralise about, something (about whose effects) one has absolutely no scruples. Not a word believed. Not a word meant. No ethics dishonestly dragged in. These are things one does for the sake of release of energy, expenditure of energy, passing time, and nothing more. They are best done when one has converted oneself into an intellectual apparatus, a centre which releases hot sparks, which has potency, which reacts to stimuli in a greater degree than other acids, minerals, chlorophylls, grooves, locomotives, etc., etc., ... in the chemico-biologico-physiological **realms.**

One does all these things for no other reason than the glorification of one's mind. Everything else can go to hell, if it can find it.

Published by the East African Publishing House, Koinange Street, P. O. Box 30571, Nairobi and printed in letterpress by afropress ltd., Saldanha Lane, P. O. Box 30502, Nairobi, Kenya.